"I have read and enjoyed the book of Esther many times over the years—both as a story and as history. Larry Christenson's presentation has given me a third reason to treasure it. I will read Esther through new eyes in the future. Prayerful eyes. I trust I will remember the many lessons on intercession that I have carried from the book as I endeavor to make them part of my own prayer life."

—**Janette Oke**, bestselling novelist; winner of
ECPA President's Award, Gold Medallion, Christy Award

"Larry Christenson is one of the best teachers I know. In *The Mantle of Esther* he demonstrates his unique genius for making theological principles alive, personal and workable. From young Esther's life-and-death adventures in the court of the powerful Persian king, he draws the biblical pattern for miracle-resulting intercession. Halfway through the book, I found myself already praying with new confidence for all the 'impossible' situations confronting our own family and friends."

—**Elizabeth Sherrill**, bestselling author of many books,
including *All the Way to Heaven: Whatever You're Facing,
Heaven Begins Now*

"Often Old Testament events in the physical realm typify spiritual principles in the New Testament, applicable for us today. The intriguing story of Esther's plea to the king on behalf of her fellow Jews illustrates both our need and the way to intercede for God's intervention in this time of great peril. Larry Christenson has unveiled from Esther's example key principles to aid us in our call to intercession. *The Mantle of Esther* is must reading for those with a burden to intercede for others and a desire for a more intimate relationship with the King of kings."

—**Dr. Morris Vaagenes**, retired pastor,
North Heights Lutheran Church, St. Paul, Minnesota

THE
MANTLE
OF
ESTHER

Discovering the Power
of Intercession

LARRY CHRISTENSON

Chosen
Grand Rapids, Michigan

Published by Chosen Books
A division of Baker Publishing Group
P.O. Box 6287, Grand Rapids, MI 49516-6287
www.chosenbooks.com

Second printing, August 2008

Printed in the United States of America

Library of Congress Cataloging-in-Publication Data
Christenson, Larry, 1928–
    The mantle of Esther : discovering the power of intercession / Larry
Christenson.
      p. cm.
    Includes bibliographical references (p.   ) and index.
    ISBN 978-0-8007-9428-6 (pbk.)
    1. Bible. O. T. Esther—Criticism, interpretation, etc. 2. Intercessory prayer.
3. Intercession. I. Title.
    BS1375.6.P68C47 2008
    248.3′2—dc22   2007036944

This book is lovingly dedicated to the memory of Helen Gates. She was in a small group the first time I taught the book of Esther as it is presented in this book. A short way into the study she said, "This is not a usual Bible study. Where did you get this?" The question caught me off guard. I had not found this approach to Esther in any book or commentary I had read. Her question forced me to say openly, "I believe it is something the Lord gave me."

Contents

Acknowledgments

My thanks to many people who have participated in seminars where I have taught the book of Esther as it is presented in this book. Their questions and suggestions have added to my appreciation of this marvelous Scripture.

My special thanks to Jane Campbell of Chosen Books who encouraged me to write the book. And to my two favorite critics whose suggestions have been invaluable: our longtime friend and colleague, a writer and editor in her own right, Dorothy Ranaghan, and my wife, Nordis, who keeps her pruning shears sharp.

Part One

PREPARATION
FOR
INTERCESSION

1

The Awesome
Sovereignty of God

Esther's story is a remarkable illustration of the ministry of intercessory prayer. In 483 B.C., as a young queen in Persia, she intervened in a dangerous situation. Her people, the Jews, were threatened with a powerful enemy bent on their destruction. Esther ventured to intercede with the king who alone could change the ominous situation. Her intercession resulted in deliverance and victory for her people.

The power of evil intrudes also in our lives. We find ourselves up against things we cannot handle or control. Under its many guises—scheming, betrayal, sickness, addiction—the power of evil seeks to trouble, harass, kill and destroy. The mantle of Esther patterns a strategy for confronting the power of evil. Esther knew from the beginning she was no match for the hateful power poised against her and her people. Step by step the unfolding story recounts how Esther enters upon a strategy to pit the power of the king against the plot of an evil enemy. In utter dependence she presents herself before the king, and there she discovers the awesome power of intercession. To this day, Jews celebrate the story of Queen Esther in the Feast of Purim. It is one of the most gripping stories in the Bible, fraught with danger, challenge and suspense. It dramatically portrays the power of effective intercession.

A "Type" of Intercessory Prayer

How do we understand the ministry of intercession? If you asked a random group of people to define *intercessory prayer*, you might receive phrases like, "Saying prayers for someone . . . presenting petitions to God . . . praying for someone else." Commonsense phrases like these are not inaccurate, but they are inadequate. We need to look more closely at how Scripture describes intercession. The Bible's portrayal of intercession is well summarized in this catechism for new believers: Intercession is a prayer of petition that leads us to pray as Jesus did. He is the one intercessor with the Father on behalf of all men, especially sinners (see Romans 8:34; 1 Timothy 2:5–8; 1 John 2:1). "He is able to save to the

> I urge that supplications, prayers, intercessions, and thanksgivings be made for all people. . . . This is good, and it is pleasing in the sight of God our Savior, who desires all people to be saved and to come to the knowledge of the truth. (1 Timothy 2:1, 3–4)

14

uttermost those who draw near to God through him, since he always lives to make intercession for them" (Hebrews 7:25). The Holy Spirit "himself intercedes for us" and "intercedes

> Intercession is a prayer of petition that leads us to pray as Jesus did.

for the saints according to the will of God" (Romans 8:26–27).[1] Intercessory prayer draws us into the presence and life of the holy Trinity where God welcomes and responds to our petitions with divine authority.

Scripture invites us to bring our intercessions before God. Solemn revelation and breathtaking promises accompany Scripture's call to intercession—

> The LORD saw it, and it displeased Him that there was no justice. He saw that there was no man, and wondered that there was no intercessor. (Isaiah 59:15–16, NKJV)

> I sought for a man among them who should build up the wall and stand in the breach before me for the land, that I should not destroy it, but I found none. Therefore I have poured out my indignation upon them. I have consumed them with the fire of my wrath. (Ezekiel 22:30–31)

> If you abide in me, and my words abide in you, ask whatever you wish, and it will be done for you. (John 15:7)

> Whatever you ask in prayer, you will receive, if you have faith. (Matthew 21:22)

> Confess your sins to one another and pray for one another, that you may be healed. The prayer of a righteous person has great power as it is working. (James 5:16)

> I urge that supplications, prayers, intercessions, and thanks-
> givings be made for all people.... This is good, and it is pleas-
> ing in the sight of God our Savior, who desires all people to
> be saved and to come to the knowledge of the truth. (1 Timo-
> thy 2:1, 3–4)

The intercessor stands between two realms, the natural and
the spiritual. Intercessory prayer brings the power of heaven
down to earth.

What can we learn about intercession from the book of
Esther? The idea of reading Esther as a "type" of intercessory
prayer came to me a long time ago. I have had the opportu-
nity to teach the book of Esther in this way at conferences,
congregations and Bible schools over more than forty years.
It has never failed to awaken both fresh confidence in a God
who answers prayer, and a renewed urgency to enter into
the ministry of intercession.

This way of approaching a Scripture is generally called
typological, something found both in the Bible itself and in
the history of biblical interpretation. Scripture frequently
presents truth in types or parables. In the Old Testament,
the marriage of Hosea and Gomer is presented as a parable
of God's "marriage" to Israel (see Hosea 1:2–3). The apostle
Paul interpreted the Old Testament story of Israel's passage
through the Red Sea as a type or prefiguring of baptism
(see 1 Corinthians 10:1–4). Jesus frequently couched His teaching in stories or parables. The parables were like handles
that helped people pick up divine truth and carry it into
everyday life. He understood the chief purpose of revelation as a guide for spiritual living, not a textbook of
divine information.

The purpose of typology is to illustrate truth, not define it. A vivid, well-chosen type may quicken fresh insight or appreciation of truth, but the truth itself is something you bring to the type "from outside." Jesus knew the truth about the future coming of God's Kingdom. He taught this truth by injecting it into stories or parables that memorably illustrated the truth. "Then the kingdom of heaven will be like ten virgins" (Matthew 25:1). "For it will be like a man going on a journey" (verse 14).

> "When the Son of Man comes in his glory, and all the angels with him, then he will sit on his glorious throne. Before him will be gathered all the nations, and he will separate people one from another as a shepherd separates the sheep from the goats." (verses 31–32)

By themselves, the parables did not define truth about the Kingdom. In Jesus' day, a woman may have watched her husband separate sheep from goats year after year and thought nothing of it. But when Jesus used that event to illustrate divine truth, a common experience became uncommonly meaningful.

When you read Scripture typologically it is important to remember that basic truth is brought to a type, not derived from it. Like a many-faceted diamond, the story of Esther reflects the truth of intercessory prayer, but is not itself the source of the teaching. A type reflects or illustrates truth; the truth itself comes from the whole of Scripture.

A type generally illustrates a particular aspect of some truth, not a point-for-point correspondence to that truth in all its details. The Old Testament, for example, presents the heathen king Cyrus as a type of Israel's savior or messiah (see Isaiah 45:1). He is not a type of messiah in everything he is and does, but specifically in his role of delivering the Jews from captivity. Like the parables that Jesus told, some aspects of a biblical type may even be contradictory to the truth being illustrated. Jesus told two parables in which He cast God the Father in unflattering roles—as a grouchy neighbor and as an unrighteous judge (see Luke 11:5–9; 18:1–8). Persistence in prayer was the point Jesus was illustrating, not the character of God. The story of Esther presents an opposite case: The king of Persia is cast in the role of God to depict divine majesty and authority; the historical details of his reign and character fall outside the typology.

The book of Esther provides the structure for our study of intercession. We do not present it as a systematic or exhaustive study of intercessory prayer. Some truths of intercessory prayer will not be mentioned because they do not come up in the story of Esther; on the other hand, the people and the unfolding events of the book will awaken fresh insights into the ministry of intercession. Think of it as a story, more to be read like a novel than a textbook. Yet it can profoundly deepen our understanding of intercessory prayer. With single-minded

> The book of Esther provides the structure for our study of intercession.

determination Esther takes to heart the plight of her people, risking everything, even life itself, to intercede before the king. Other characters in the story fulfill typological roles that further illustrate the practice of intercession. Across the

> The people and the unfolding events of the book will awaken fresh insights into the ministry of intercession.

centuries, the story of Esther has spoken strong encouragement to those who feel called into the presence of the Lord to pray on behalf of others.

Background of the Book of Esther

The Jewish people have long considered the story of Esther peculiarly sacred. The annual Feast of Purim, rooted in the book of Esther, is one of the most joyful celebrations in the Jewish religious calendar. The book of Esther raises some questions when one first begins to study it. It appears to be a rather secular book. God's name is never mentioned. It is never quoted in the New Testament. It contains no references to prayer, or any sacred observances.

Its place in the Old Testament canon, however, has never come seriously into question because it is an evident part of "holy history," the working out of God's plan of salvation in human history. It is a modern tendency to let ideology or abstract principles trump history. If something does not measure up to, or fit in with, a principle or idea we currently hold, the offending practice stands in danger of being swept aside. Henry Halley grasps the heart of this issue in his comment:

The book of Esther is about a Very Important Historical Event, not just a story to point out a moral: The Hebrew Nation's Deliverance from Annihilation in the days following the Babylonian Captivity. If the Hebrew Nation had been entirely wiped out of existence 500 years before it brought Christ into the world, that might have made some difference in God's plans and in the destiny of mankind: no Hebrew Nation, no Messiah: no Messiah, a lost world. This beautiful Jewish girl of the long ago, though she herself may not have known it, yet played her part in paving the way for the coming of the world's Saviour.[2]

Esther is set in a particular period of the history of Israel: during Israel's defeat and captivity, after Jerusalem fell to the armies of Babylon in 586 B.C. Subsequently, the Medes and Persians conquered the Babylonian kingdom. It was during this period of Persian rule that the book of Esther takes place. In a biblical context it would fall roughly between the sixth and seventh chapters of the book of Ezra. The Temple has been rebuilt. The wall of Jerusalem is not yet built. G. Campbell Morgan, a great expositor of Scripture, suggests that Persian documents form the basic resource for the book of Esther.[3] This finds support in the book of Esther itself: In the final chapter we read that the basic elements of the story were "written in the Book of the Chronicles of the kings of Media and Persia" (Esther 10:2). The absence of a reference to God, or to religious observances, in Esther actually corresponds to its

> Across the centuries, the story of Esther has spoken strong encouragement to those who feel called into the presence of the Lord to pray on behalf of others.

theme—the providence of God in response to the plight of His people. The providence of God is often visible only to the eyes of faith. It may not register with a person who simply views a historical situation from the outside. The story itself is a compelling narrative, one of the most dramatic in Scripture.

> The absence of a reference to God, or to religious observances, in Esther actually corresponds to its theme—the providence of God in response to the plight of His people.

The Majesty of the King

> Now in the days of Ahasuerus, the Ahasuerus who reigned from India to Ethiopia over 127 provinces, in those days when King Ahasuerus sat on his royal throne in Susa, the capital, in the third year of his reign he gave a feast for all his officials and servants. (Esther 1:1–3)

The literal meaning of *Ahasuerus* is "king" and is the Jewish name by which he is known in the book of Esther. His Persian name, by which he is known in world history, is Xerxes, which means "chief of rulers." In the typology of intercession, he serves as a type of God, or of Christ the King, or of Christ the Bridegroom (other literal details of his life and character are not relevant to the typological role, which is true of the other characters as well). He represents God's sovereign rule, God's providence over all things.

To focus first of all on the sovereign majesty of God highlights an aspect of intercession often skipped over. In a rush to tell people about the love of God, our imagery for God often becomes one-sidedly intimate, personal or simply sentimental. A wag in Australia said, "We have changed the Apostles' Creed to read, 'I believe in God the Father all-matey.'" A biblical sense of awe and adoration loses traction if our understanding of God gets stuck at buddy-buddy.

Serious intercession tilts the imagery back toward reverence, keenly aware that in intercession even urgent personal concerns assume a secondary role. Esther comes into the king's presence with humility and awe, knowing that a great matter is at stake, and only the king's sovereign power can deal with it. The ministry of intercession begins by reckoning realistically with God's authority over all things. All things and all people are subject to His rule. On this truth hinges the power of intercession.

Another story in Scripture presents both similarities and contrasts to Esther's story, yet illustrates the same theme of God's sovereignty—the book of Job. When Job had gone through many sufferings, he remonstrated with God: "Oh, that I knew where I might find him, that I might come even to his seat! I would lay my case before him and fill my mouth with arguments" (Job 23:3–4). God responds first by reminding Job of the Creation. He recounts for him the power with which He created the entire universe. Job, sitting on an ash heap, scratching away at the painful boils that afflict him, concedes, "I know that you can

> To focus first of all on the sovereign majesty of God highlights an aspect of intercession often skipped over. In a rush to tell people about the love of God, our imagery for God often becomes one-sidedly intimate, personal or simply sentimental.

do all things, and that no purpose of yours can be thwarted" (Job 42:2). You half expect Job to add, "But what about poor me?" God goes on, showing Job the things He has made: Leviathan, the great sea creatures, the places where He stores the hail and the snow. He portrays for Job the absolute sovereignty with which He runs the whole universe. And Job can do nothing but recognize and admit it.

Then comes the turning point in God's revelation and Job's understanding. It enters so inconspicuously you could almost miss it. As Job sits in agony—scratch, scratch, scratch—God begins to describe the hippopotamus. "Look at the hippopotamus! Isn't he powerful? Look at the strength of his legs!" Can you imagine any man in Job's situation summoning up sudden delight in a blubbery hippopotamus? Job has suffered loss after loss, unimaginable physical distress, and what does God do? Invites him, in the midst of it all, to take delight in the hippopotamus. God goes into rhapsody over this creature He has made. Then He throws in the little phrase, "Whom I made . . . *as I made you.*" And it dawns on Job: "If God so loves the . . . hippopotamus . . . then surely He loves me as well."

That is the other side of God's sovereignty. His sovereignty is perfectly wedded to His love. When Job sensed that God loved him as surely as He loved the hippopotamus, he was content. The great question hovering over the book of Job, "Why do the righteous suffer?" is never answered. But Job entered into a greater truth: This awesome, powerful God, who created all things . . . made me and loves me.

These same two themes thread through the story of Esther: the awesome sovereignty of God, matched to tender and

> God's sovereignty is perfectly wedded to His love.

powerful love. But the focus falls first of all, as it did for Job, on the awesome sovereignty of God. Anyone who wants to become an intercessor must first of all embrace the truth of God's absolute sovereignty. All things—including this urgent intercession that presently lies on my heart—must come with awe into the presence of God, and kneel before His majesty. When people declaim, "How can a loving God allow a tornado to destroy a whole town, killing hundreds of innocent people? How can a loving God allow cancer to take the life of this mother with three small children?"—they come at the problem backward. They fault God for allowing something bad to happen without first presenting the thing before Him. The Bible does not treat the presence of evil in simplistic terms, something a loving God should simply prevent or sweep away. Evil is a malevolent force that seeks to separate us from God. The first step in dealing with evil is to draw near to God.

The story of Esther illustrates the centrality of this truth in an unforgettable way: In chapter four we will see that Esther ventures to intercede with the king at the risk of her life. If the king does not receive her, the result is not simply an unanswered petition; it is death. Esther teaches more than an abstract doctrine of God's sovereignty; she teaches us an attitude of humility and reverence that can spell the difference between intercession that fails and intercession that triumphs.

This theme of God's sovereignty is threaded through Scripture and experience. In the book of Ephesians, sometimes called "a blueprint of the church," the apostle Paul extols the awesome sovereignty of God. Ten times, in less than a dozen verses, he repeats and elaborates on the theme that God "works all things according to the counsel of his will" (see Ephesians 1:3–14). The healing evangelist Kathryn Kuhlman once wrote in *Christianity Today* that one of the most agonizing moments she experienced during her ministry was when she watched unhealed people leave the meeting. When people were healed and came forward to give their testimony, it was a time of great rejoicing. But then she watched those who were not healed trudge away, and she asked, "Lord, why?" even though she knew no answer would come. She did as Job did, bowed before the awesome sovereignty of God, acknowledging that despite every negative circumstance, God's love is sure.

The Wisdom of God

> On the seventh day, when the heart of the king was merry with wine, he commanded Mehuman, Biztha, Harbona, Bigtha and Abagtha, Zethar and Carkas, the seven eunuchs who served in the presence of King Ahasuerus, to bring Queen Vashti before the king with her royal crown, in order to show the peoples and the princes her beauty, for she was lovely to look at. (Esther 1:10–11)

The seven eunuchs were the king's servants, ministers to do his bidding. Their names suggest how richly textured is the obedience due the sovereign authority of the king. *Mehuman*

These same two themes thread through the story of Esther: the awesome sovereignty of God, matched to tender and powerful love.

25

comes from the same root as the word *Amen!* and means "firm, steady, true; a faithful servant of his master." He is spokesman for the advisers, giving voice to their obedience. *Biztha* is related to the idea of "plunder," the winnings of warfare; here it is obedience to do battle and return booty to the king. *Bigtha* means "something given by fortune, a gift of God"; obedience is no drear duty, but that for which he was made. *Abagtha* means "happy" or "prosperous"; obedience to the king shapes his attitudes and feelings, crowns his life with success. *Zethar* means "one who slays, a smiter, or sacrifice"; the call to obedience can be ruthless, cutting through human pretensions, performing surgery on warped human notions. *Carkas* means "severe"; the word of the king may not always be pleasant to hear, may be stern, demanding.

One of the advisors has a name that is somewhat puzzling. *Harbona* means "an ass driver" or "a baldheaded man." He is like a country bumpkin. A baldheaded man in Scripture was the occasion for jest. When Elisha came back from having seen Elijah taken up to heaven in a fiery chariot, some children came out of the woods and made fun of him: "Go up, you baldhead! Go up, you baldhead" (2 Kings 2:23). Apparently they meant, "Why don't you go and do what Elijah did, old baldy?" They made fun of Elisha's vivid religious experience. Walking in obedience to God may bring ridicule down on our heads. We may be mocked or misunderstood by those who shrug off the

> The seven eunuchs were the king's servants, ministers to do his bidding. Their names suggest how richly textured is the obedience due the sovereign authority of the king.

plan or purpose of God. But keep an eye on Harbona, as the plot thickens! At a critical moment in the story he illustrates a heartening truth about intercession.

The sovereignty of God is wedded to His wisdom. Charles Simpson, one of the wisest pastors I have known in my life, with an uncommon gift of humor, put it this way: "If something is wrong and God does it, it's right!" Mother Basilea, founder of the Evangelical Sisterhood of Mary in Darmstadt, Germany, framed it as a prayer: "Father, I don't understand You, but I trust You." Queen Vashti throws the theme of sovereignty into stark relief by challenging the rightness of the king's request. The word *Vashti* means "a beautiful woman." She represents one with a special calling. She sits beside the king. She is summoned "on the seventh day, when the heart of the king was merry with wine. . . . But Queen Vashti refused to come at the king's command delivered by the eunuchs" (Esther 1:10, 12). The king summoned the queen at his pleasure, at a time of his choosing, but she declined to come. The call of God does not always come at a time that feels right to us, or is convenient for us. We may hesitate, complaining that the call is inappropriate or demands more of us than we are ready to give. We may pause or draw back. In effect, we are tempted to set our wisdom above His wisdom, our authority above His.

In a book titled *Realities*, the Evangelical Sisters of Mary recounted how Mother Basilea once came to them with a vision that they were to build a "Jesus Proclamation Chapel." They had just completed some other buildings and had, as it

> The call of God does not always come at a time that feels right to us, or is convenient for us.

were, worn themselves out in prayer. Now came this call to prayer that was beyond anything they had attempted up until then. They grumbled that they were too weary to undertake another prayer project, too exhausted to go through another battle of faith. Yet, when they repented of their grumbling, God refreshed their faith. They watched thousands of people stream into the Jesus Proclamation Chapel where their vivid chancel dramas portrayed the Gospel message, and their call for Germany's repentance toward the Jews gained a wide hearing. When you enter the ministry of intercession, you are "on call" for God—not at your convenience, but when *His* moment arrives, when "*His* heart is merry." The life and hope of the intercessor is built on the foundation of God's sovereign authority, wisdom and power. The intercessor kneels humbly before that sovereignty, for only by that sovereign power will the hate-filled power of evil be defeated.

The first scene in Esther's story ends on a sobering note. When Queen Vashti refused the king's summons, "the king became enraged, and his anger burned within him" (Esther 1:12). God takes our relationship with Him more seriously

> God takes our relationship with Him more seriously than we do.

than we do. The Holy Spirit sometimes asks that which seems inconvenient to us; when the call of God comes, the temptation to draw back may be roused in us. God does not look on indulgently if we draw back.

He becomes enraged. Jesus told the story of a king who had prepared a wedding banquet for his son. Those who were invited "paid no attention and went off, one to his farm, another to his business" (Matthew 22:5). The king was enraged. He said, "The

> In effect, we are tempted to set our wisdom above His wisdom, our authority above His.

wedding feast is ready, but those invited were not worthy. Go therefore to the main roads and invite to the wedding feast as many as you find" (verses 8–9). When God sends out a call, it is because in His awesome sovereignty He has decided what He wants done. One called to be an intercessor is like a doctor on 24-hour call. He does not set "office hours" when he will be available to God. He is available to God whenever God, in His wisdom, determines intercession is called for.

> Then the king said to the wise men who knew the times (for this was the king's procedure toward all who were versed in law and judgment, the men next to him being Carshena, Shethar, Admatha, Tarshish, Meres, Marsena, and Memucan, the seven princes of Persia and Media, who saw the king's face, and sat first in the kingdom): "According to the law, what is to be done to Queen Vashti, because she has not performed the command of King Ahasuerus delivered by the eunuchs?" (Esther 1:13–15)

According to Ezra 7:14, these were the counselors who brought their wisdom to bear on a variety of questions the king presented to them. We do not always understand God's ways. The apostle Paul said that sometimes the wisdom of

> Wisdom accords with God's character, purpose and standard of righteousness.

God comes across as foolishness to human reason (see 1 Corinthians 1:25). The names of the king's counselors are interesting. They suggest the diverse and even paradoxical nature of divine wisdom. The name *Carshena* means "lean, slender." True wisdom does not need a waterfall of speech; divine and precise, it can be sparing with words. *Shethar* means "star, commander." Wisdom is linked to authority. When Jesus taught, the common people "were astonished at his teaching, for he taught them as one who had authority, and not as the scribes" (Mark 1:22). *Admatha* means "God-given." This is the ultimate characteristic of true wisdom. Jesus said, "I do nothing on my own authority, but speak just as the Father taught me" (John 8:28). *Tarshish* means "hard." Wisdom that comes against our settled human ways may come across as hard and unfeeling. *Meres* and *Marsena* both mean "worthy." Wisdom accords with God's character, purpose and standard of righteousness. *Memucan*, the spokesman for the seven counselors, means "authority, dignity." True wisdom stands above petty human squabbles. It sends vain arguments and pretentious posturing into shamed retreat.

Some have tried to intrude a contemporary contention into the story, declaring Vashti's rebellion an appropriate assertion of feminine authority and independence against a dissolute male authority who perhaps wanted to parade her naked before a drunken throng. The text gives no hint of such a notion. The matter is judged in more radical terms. The issue at stake is the queen's choosing to act independently of the sovereign king. In the typology of the story, it is a believer putting his or her own judgment above the call of the Lord. The wise men say that Vashti has not only offended the king, she has set a bad example for all the homes in the kingdom. Women are going to rebel against their husbands because Queen Vashti has rebelled against the king. The counselors of the king are "men who know the times." They know that rebellion and strife in the homes will spawn times of disorder in the kingdom. When you read the qualifications for church leaders in the New Testament (see 1 Timothy 3:2–5, 12; Titus 1:6–9), it is clear that the health and stability of the church rests upon well-ordered homes.

The intercessor reckons realistically with the wisdom of God's will and purpose. When God wanted to put something on earth that was like Himself, He "created man in his own image, in the image of God he created him; male and female he created them" (Genesis 1:27). In this very first description of humankind in Scripture, it is clear that the "image of God" finds expression not only in individuals but also in the intimate relationship of husband and wife, the creation of human beings as male and female. How much of the rebellion we see in the world is encouraged, or goes unchallenged, because God's people have set a bad example, have moved away from their God-ordained calling of "representing Him on earth"? In our churches, and in our families, have we manifested a spirit of rebellion

> The issue at stake is the queen's choosing to act independently of the sovereign king. In the typology of the story, it is a believer putting his or her own judgment above the call of the Lord.

31

The intercessor reckons realistically with the wisdom of God's will and purpose.

---

that plays to the world's sinful disdain of authority?

Whether we realize it or not, whether we like it or not, we are a witness in the world—for good or for ill. If we manifest a spirit of self-will, a spirit of independence and rebellion, the world will pick that up. We will see demonstrations of rebellion that will shock us, yet we never stop to consider to what extent we have failed to live out our God-ordained calling to represent Him on earth. If a good witness for God can have a wholesome effect in the world, then we have to reckon with the counterpart, that a poor witness will also impact the world. Perhaps we should not be surprised if God brings judgment first of all upon families in the church: "For it is time for judgment to begin at the household of God" (1 Peter 4:17). Humbling judgment must often precede being used and useful to the Lord.

The counselors to King Ahasuerus recognized that the homes of the whole realm were endangered because of the bad example set by the queen. The advisers counsel that Vashti should be set aside, and another queen be sought to take her place. This is the somber note on which the first chapter in the story of Esther concludes. If we back off from the call of God, the plan of God will go forward, but we can be set aside. Someone else will be called

---

If a good witness for God can have a wholesome effect in the world, then we have to reckon with the counterpart, that a poor witness will also impact the world.

---

forward to do the job God wanted us to do. It is not a question of losing one's salvation, as such, but of losing one's call. If we refuse God's gracious invitation to exercise a ministry He has given us, or that He wants to give us, we may find the judgment of the Lord excluding us from ministry. To be set aside by God—*a deeply troubling thought!* The lesson of Vashti will not be lost on Esther. As the story unfolds, Esther learns that the awesome sovereignty of the king is her first consideration and the key to successful intercession.

This is the somber note on which the first chapter in the story of Esther concludes.

If we back off from the call of God, the plan of God will go forward, but we can be set aside. Someone else will be called forward to do the job God wanted us to do.

33

2

The Training of an Intercessor

After these things, when the anger of King Ahasuerus had abated, he remembered Vashti and what she had done and what had been decreed against her. Then the king's young men who attended him said, "Let beautiful young virgins be sought out for the king. And let the king appoint officers in all the provinces of his kingdom to gather all the beautiful young virgins to the harem in Susa the capital, under custody of Hegai, the king's eunuch, who is in charge of the women. Let their cosmetics be given them. And let the young woman who pleases the king be queen instead of Vashti." This pleased the king, and he did so. (Esther 2:1–4)

Esther was one of the young women summoned to the king's palace. She had nothing to do with the events that brought her there. She was suddenly caught up in things beyond her, over which she had no control. Whatever personal plans she may have had were set aside. The ministry of intercession thrusts the will of God into the center of our lives, calling for a radical reordering of our priorities. The narrow horizon of our own needs and plans gives way to the purposes of the Kingdom. The controlling concern for the intercessor becomes simply, "What does the Lord desire of me? How may I please Him?"

Esther was an orphan. She had been raised by her elderly cousin, Mordecai. As the story unfolds, Mordecai senses acutely the peril of his people. Mordecai represents Christ as he identifies with the reproach and suffering of God's people. Mordecai is from the tribe of Benjamin, neighbor to the tribe of Judah, which was designated to rule: "The scepter shall not depart from Judah, nor the ruler's staff from between his feet" (Genesis 49:10). In the story of Esther, God's people move through endangerment and suffering to ultimate triumph. The pathway to spiritual honor and authority passes through the valley of suffering.

> The ministry of intercession thrusts the will of God into the center of our lives, calling for a radical reordering of our priorities.

Mordecai's genealogy is interesting. He is from the family of Jair, which means "the Lord enlightens," the family of Shimei, which means "the Lord is fame," and of the family of Kish, which means "power." The heritage in each of these names comes into play as the story unfolds.

Esther's Jewish name is Hadassah. The name means "myrtle" and evokes remembrance of high festival, of rejoicing and thanksgiving. Myrtle was one of the plants used to build temporary shelters in the fields during the Feast of Booths, the high celebration of bringing in the harvest. Her Persian name, Esther, means

> The controlling concern for the intercessor becomes simply, "What does the Lord desire of me? How may I please Him?"

"star of the east." It brings to mind the account of the wise men visiting Bethlehem at the birth of Jesus: "Where is He who has been born King of the Jews? For we have seen His star in the East and have come to worship Him" (Matthew 2:2, NKJV). It is also memorialized in the Epiphany hymnody of the church—

> Brightest and best of the sons of the morning,
> Dawn on our darkness and lend us thine aid;
> Star of the east, the horizon adorning,
> Guide where our infant Redeemer is laid.

Profile of an Intercessor

In the Bible, Esther's father and mother are absent. Her orphan upbringing significantly shaped her life, yet she came to the palace chosen by the king as an individual, not because of family or group attachments. "God Has No Grandsons!" was the title of a tract by David du Plessis, famed Pentecostal ambassador to historic Protestant and Catholic churches in the latter half of the twentieth century. *We become children of God by direct generation, not because of family or denominational association.* When Jesus said, "Whoever does the will of God, he is my brother and sister and mother" (Mark 3:35), He was setting aside any notion that authentic spiritual life comes simply by belonging to some family or group. Growing up in a Christian family, belonging to a Christian fellowship, is a marked privilege and can significantly shape one's life, but it does not of itself beget spiritual life or make one a candidate for ministry. One called to be an intercessor must first of all be one whom God invites into His presence because he or she belongs to Him through personal faith in Jesus, the divine Son of God.

> [Esther] had a beautiful figure and was lovely to look at.
> (Esther 2:7)

The question for Esther was whether the king's favor would fall on her, whether she would be attractive to him. Her charm and appeal is typological of a believer whose life is pleasing to God. Jesus modeled such a life, and said, "I always do the things that are pleasing to him" (John 8:29). The apostle John echoed this for followers of Jesus: "We keep his commandments and do what pleases him" (1 John 3:22). It was likewise the prayer of the apostle Paul when he wrote, "Walk in a manner worthy of the Lord, fully pleasing to him" (Colossians 1:10). The initial, and indeed the controlling, concern of the intercessor is always this: How may I please the Lord?

We become children of God by direct generation, not because of family or denominational association.

The intercessor, driven by this concern to please the Lord, models for the church the image of a Bride "without spot or wrinkle or any such thing, that she might be holy and without blemish" (Ephesians 5:27). Intercessors see beyond the immediate situation. They lay claim to the promises of God on behalf of others. They live, as it were, more in the book of Ephesians, which is focused on the purposes of God, than in Corinthians, which is focused on the problems of people. Not that they stand aloof from human problems; quite the contrary. But they see beyond. They project the church beyond the present situation, boldly interceding for the supernatural intervention of God.

> Intercessors see beyond the immediate situation. They lay claim to the promises of God on behalf of others.

The Intercessor in Training

> Esther also was taken into the king's palace and put in custody of Hegai, who had charge of the women. And the young woman pleased him and won his favor. (Esther 2:8–9)

Hegai prepares Esther for her meeting with the king. His name means "festive." The training will be demanding but not burdensome, for the goal is highly prized: to be received and found pleasing by the king. In the typology of the story, Hegai represents the Holy Spirit. The Holy Spirit trains intercessors for ministry that goes far beyond merely "saying prayers" or "reciting petitions." He prepares them to please the Lord, something for which the natural person has no inborn talent. What first of all pleases the Holy Spirit and finds favor with Him are believers who are teachable: They

39

want to live so as to please God, but do not presume to know how. He takes them under His wing and begins to impart to them a new way of thinking and living.

> You must no longer walk as the Gentiles do, in the futility of their minds. They are darkened in their understanding, alienated from the life of God because of the ignorance that is in them, due to their hardness of heart. . . . Put off your old self, which belongs to your former manner of life and is corrupt through deceitful desires, and to be renewed in the spirit of your minds . . . put on the new self, created after the likeness of God in true righteousness and holiness.
> (Ephesians 4:17–18, 22–24)

The training of the Holy Spirit is no mere schooling in techniques of prayer. He imparts the way of life into which we are adopted, the life of the Holy Trinity.

Esther's reverent behavior toward the king is inherent in the story. From the moment she comes to the palace, she regards the king with the greatest awe and respect. In the typology of intercession, Esther challenges the decline of reverence that has come to dominate much of contemporary Christian worship. The Lord Himself—who He is and what He has done—is often displaced by how I think and feel about God, which greatly weakens the ministry

> What first of all pleases the Holy Spirit and finds favor with Him are believers who are teachable: They want to live so as to please God, but do not presume to know how.

40

of intercession. Instead of "What a Friend We Have in Jesus" or "When I Survey the Wondrous Cross," we charge into God's presence chanting, "I am a friend of God! I think about Him day and night! I am desperate for Him! My love for Him knows no bounds!" Derek Prince makes a similar point: "In Psalm 95:6–7 we get to the heart of the matter: 'Come, let us bow down in worship, let us kneel

> Esther's reverent behavior toward the king is inherent in the story. From the moment she comes to the palace, she regards the king with the greatest awe and respect.

before the LORD our Maker (NIV).' As I see it, this purposeful worship is not the type of loud boisterousness that has become the norm; it is quietness."[1] Hegai's preparation of Esther has no other goal than her intimate encounter with the king. But it is not an intimacy of shallow, self-absorbed familiarity. It is the intimacy of reverence, humbly entering into and responding to the concerns and pleasure of the king.

When Jesus taught His disciples to pray, "Our Father in heaven," He immediately followed with, "hallowed be your name," which carries the meaning, "let your name be treated with reverence" (see Matthew 6:9 footnote). The invitation to call God "Father," or even more intimately "Abba," is not an invitation to easy familiarity that parades our feelings, ideas, petitions and preferences around in God's presence. Jesus taught His disciples that confident access to God as *Father* is twin to a reverent regard for God's purpose and will: "*Your* kingdom come, *your* will be done." Jesus Himself underscored the awe and respect for God's will that must

41

Jesus taught His disciples that confident access to God as *Father* is twin to a reverent regard for God's purpose and will.

accompany effective intercession. In Gethsemane He prayed, "Abba, Father, all things are possible for you. Remove this cup from me. Yet not what I will, but what you will" (Mark 14:36). The Father's plan of salvation hung on that final sentence in Jesus' prayer. Reverence is more than an intellectual formula ascribing first place to God's will. It is an awe-filled attitude that waits patiently on God, intent to discern and enter into His will.

Hegai knows exactly how to prepare Esther for her audience with the king. He provides everything needed during her time of preparation.

[Hegai] quickly provided her [Esther] with her cosmetics and her portion of food, and with seven chosen young women from the king's palace, and advanced her and her young women to the best place in the harem. (Esther 2:9)

Reverence is more than an intellectual formula ascribing first place to God's will. It is an awe-filled attitude that waits patiently on God, intent to discern and enter into His will.

Cosmetics ... food ... seven young women, chosen resources to help prepare Esther for her audience with the king. The centerpiece in the intercessor's preparation is the Word of God. Receiving "her portion of food" corresponds to receiving spiritual nourishment, and so to Holy Scripture. "Long for the pure spiritual milk, that by it you may grow up into salvation" (1 Peter 2:2).

Experience of the supernatural can be heady. And it can be deceptive, causing a person to veer off course. Precisely because the intercessor may have powerful experiences, and may be called to demonstrate the power of God, experience must be held humbly subject to the written Word. "All Scripture is breathed out by God and profitable for teaching, for reproof, for correction, and for training in

> The ministry of intercession is not based on wispy spiritual feelings, nor even powerful experiences, but on instruction in the truth and reality of Scripture.

righteousness" (2 Timothy 3:16). The ministry of intercession is not based on wispy spiritual feelings, nor even powerful experiences, but on instruction in the truth and reality of Scripture. "Present yourself to God as one approved, a worker who has no need to be ashamed, rightly handling the word of truth" (2 Timothy 2:15).

Closely linked to the intercessor's dependence on Scripture is respectful regard for the teaching ministry of the church. The call to intercession is a call to enter into the fellowship of God's people, there to be taught and prepared. Prepared not simply for a task, but prepared as a person. The Holy Spirit includes wholesome instruction in God's Word to nourish and maintain a life being prepared for the ministry of intercession.

Besides her portions of food, Hegai provides Esther with cosmetics to enhance her beauty. Spiritual beauty suggests godly behavior. The schooling of an intercessor does not focus simply on helpful hints about prayer but on the beauty of a transformed life and character. Spiritual beauty comes to blossom in God-pleasing behavior. The adorning of a godly woman is "the hidden person of the heart with the imperishable beauty of a gentle and quiet spirit, which in God's sight is very precious" (1 Peter 3:4). Scripture calls husbands to a life transformed by the power of Christ: "Love your wives, as Christ loved the church and gave himself up for her" (Ephesians 5:25). In the end time vision of the apostle John, it was granted the Bride of the Lamb "to clothe herself with fine linen, bright and pure—for the fine linen is the righteous deeds of the saints" (Revelation 19:8). The ministry of intercession grows out of one's personal relationship with the Lord. Seen in its entirety, intercession is simply an occasion in the life of one made beautiful, who lives to please God.

The ministry of intercession can at times be a lonely calling, yet intercessors are not loners. When the intercessor comes into the presence of God, great power may be released. Yet that which accompanies intercession is neither a sense of isolation nor of power and self-sufficiency, but a heightened bond of attachment to others. The New Testament knows nothing of lone wolf Christians. Both in the preparation and performance of intercession, the intercessor depends upon the help of other believers. Seven chosen young women from the king's palace assist Esther in her preparation. As Esther's story unfolds, they share in her intercession. In Scripture, seven suggests fullness or completeness. Seven lamps provided light for the tabernacle in the wilderness, according to the detailed

> The schooling of an intercessor does not focus simply on helpful hints about prayer but on the beauty of a transformed life and character.

44

instructions God gave Moses (see Exodus 25:37). The worship of God does not reach fulfillment in light of one or two stark principles, but under cover of seven lights, representing a fullness of revelation. When you have learned, for example, the truth

> Intercessors must become steeped in the story, statutes and promises of God's Word. It takes time.

of salvation, that is a wonderful truth to share with others. But a relationship with God does not end with the assurance of salvation. It has been well said by Lutheran pastor Delbert Rossin, "There is nothing more to salvation than Jesus, but there is more to Jesus than salvation." Scripture instructs believers to "leave the elementary doctrine of Christ and go on to maturity" (Hebrews 6:1). Intercessors must become steeped in the story, statutes and promises of God's Word. It takes time.

According to the instruction of Mordecai, Esther was to live for a time in secret. Hegai's plan in the palace also called for a time of seclusion.

> Esther had not made known her people or kindred, for Mordecai had commanded her not to make it known. And every day Mordecai walked in front of the court of the harem to learn how Esther was and what was happening to her.
> (Esther 2:10–11)

Ministry in the Body of Christ moves through different phases. Our thoughts about ministry gravitate naturally to active ministry—"going out," "witnessing in the street," "spiritual warfare." The prelude to active ministry, however, is often a protected time of nurture, training and strengthening. You

> The prelude to active ministry is often a protected time of nurture, training and strengthening.

would not send a troop of Boy Scouts into a battle that required hardened combat soldiers. There is a time for going out, but it is often linked to a time of unobserved preparation.

God is well acquainted with the enemy's vicious strategy against new life: ruthless opposition with a view to extermination. An oak tree can be exterminated—pulled out by its roots with two fingers—when it first breaks the surface. But when the oak has grown a sturdy trunk and root system it will not be easily moved. For a time God extends His hand of protection over new life. He protected young David from the death-dealing schemes of King Saul. He secluded the infant Jesus from the murderous savagery of King Herod. The church must guard against catapulting young converts into situations for which they are unprepared. Caution: This cannot be framed as a rigid principle; the Lord may do surprising things in and through the lives of new believers. Yet the fellowship of believers is cautioned to "not be hasty in the laying on of hands" (1 Timothy 5:22), quickly pushing new believers into ministry for which they are unprepared. Like a mother and father, the church has responsibility to protect, shelter and nurture new life until it gains knowledge and strength to cope with adult responsibilities.

> There is a time for going out, but it is often linked to a time of unobserved preparation.

As a type of intercessory prayer, Esther's story suggests that an intercessor becomes subject to orderly authority. The ministry of intercession is intimately and organically related

46

to the life of the church, a truth abundantly testified to in Scripture (see, for example, Ephesians 6:18–19).

> Before a girl's turn came to go in to King Xerxes [Ahasuerus], she had to complete twelve months of beauty treatments prescribed for the women, six months with oil of myrrh and six with perfumes and cosmetics. (Esther 2:12, NIV)

As a type of intercessory prayer, Esther's story suggests that an intercessor becomes subject to orderly authority.

In Scripture, the number twelve suggests order and government; for example, the elders of the twelve tribes of Israel who made a covenant and anointed David king over Israel (see 2 Samuel 5:1–3), the twelve apostles who will sit on twelve thrones of judgment (see Matthew 19:28). If our prayer is purely vertical, if it is rooted only in our own relationship to God, and our current grasp of that relationship, its breadth and depth will be stunted, its power diminished. The king takes it for granted that Esther has been prepared when she comes into his presence. The prayers of an intercessor mature and draw strength through training that accords with the order of the kingdom.

Some years ago I went through a personal struggle in regard to the doctrine of baptism. One of the things that helped me during this time was the fact that I was related to the structure of the church. I had read Karl Barth's small book *The Church's Ministry of Baptism*, in which he argues against the practice of infant baptism. I was a young, inexperienced pastor, and Karl Barth is a persuasive arguer. I had no ready answers for the kind of questions he raised. Yet, as a Lutheran pastor, I continued to baptize children according to the practice of our church. The order, structure and historical understanding of my church gave me a place to stand, and to grow, through a time when my own thoughts were turbulent and in flux.

Preparation for ministry grafts us into the life of God's people. We begin to learn and be shaped by an accumulation of wisdom that we do not yet personally possess. It does not happen overnight. The preparation prescribed for Esther continued for twelve months, six months with myrrh and six months with perfumes and cosmetics. Both of these suggest a time of patient preparation for ministry. Paradoxically, myrrh also suggests preparation for death. If a ministry of intercession is to become truly powerful, the intercessor must inevitably become subject to a process of crucifixion and death. The apostle Paul wrote, "I die every day!" (1 Corinthians 15:31). In another place he elaborated on the same thought: "We . . . are always being given over to death for Jesus' sake" (2 Corinthians 4:11). He was not talking about physical death but about the "death" of his own plans, his own ambitions and his own desires. God had revealed to him the mystery that out of his "death" God would supernaturally work life in others. "So death is at work in us, but life in you" (verse 12). The intercessor's life in the presence of God is rooted in the miracle of sharing in Christ's death and resurrection, coming before Him with Christ's own standing before the Father.

> The intercessor's life in the presence of God is rooted in the miracle of sharing in Christ's death and resurrection, coming before Him with Christ's own standing before the Father.

48

We were buried therefore with him by baptism into death, in order that, just as Christ was raised from the dead by the glory of the Father, we too might walk in newness of life. . . . So you also must consider yourselves dead to sin and alive to God in Christ Jesus. (Romans 6:4, 11)

Trusting Hegai

When the young woman went in to the king in this way, she was given whatever she desired to take with her. . . . When the turn came for Esther . . . to go in to the king, she asked for nothing except what Hegai . . . advised. (Esther 2:13, 15)

I love this in Esther. She took into the king's presence only what Hegai told her to take. The name of Esther's father, Abihail, means "father of might." Even though she was beautiful, Esther did not count on the strength of her natural endowments when she came into the presence of the king. She wisely trusted herself to Hegai's advice and care. We easily fall into depending upon some natural talent for ministry—say, a gift for eloquence that we might use in intercession, or a capacity for compassion, or a reputation for knowledge and wisdom. God may call some natural endowment into His service, but in themselves these endowments are simply available.

For 22 years I served as pastor of a congregation in California. Some years later the congregation was without a pastor; they asked me to come and serve in the interim and assist them in the process of calling a new pastor. Our original time in the congregation had been eventful. It was one of the first Lutheran congregations to become involved in the emerging charismatic movement and had experienced marked spiritual awakening, particularly in prayer, Bible study and renewal of family life. Shortly after our current arrival one of the newer members, who knew us only by name, said, "You come here with a lot of 'pastoral capital.'" Another member reported a comment from a meeting of the church council after we had accepted the call as interim pastor: "What do you think it will be: Reunion Cruise or Boot Camp?"

It was true that we were returning to very familiar territory, to the memory of things God had done among us, to friends with whom we had shared life-changing experiences. It would have been easy simply to rehearse or try to reignite the past. But while we were still back home, packing up for our trip to California, a thought had come to me one morning during my prayers: *You are not called to do much admonishing or correcting. Your time there will be too short. God Himself will deal with people's personal needs. You are to preach and teach the Word and pray.* My personal journal, from just a few weeks after our arrival, carries this entry: "The Lord is definitely leading us. I don't know how much, or exactly what He has on the drawing board for the time we are here, but I'll say this: I can't remember a time when I have been so involved or caught up in a sense of His guidance, direction and initiative."

> The ministry of intercession calls for a keen sense of *Kingdom.* The intercessor has but one hope, and it is fastened on the purpose, authority and power of God.

As the months unfolded, it became clear that the Lord had in mind

50

neither a reunion cruise nor a charismatic boot camp, but rather, a patient and sometimes painful Spirit-led process of working through certain things that were new to me and to the congregation, and preparing the congregation to receive the ministry of the new pastor whom He had chosen. The ministry of intercession depends fundamentally on the presence, power and, above all, the guidance of the Holy Spirit.

The ministry of intercession calls for a keen sense of *Kingdom*. The intercessor has but one hope, and it is fastened on the purpose, authority and power of God. Further, the Holy Spirit directs the intercessor into Kingdom ministry according to the wisdom, timing and choice that is appropriate to the Kingdom.

> Esther was taken to King Ahasuerus, into his royal palace, in the tenth month . . . in the seventh year of his reign.
> (Esther 2:16)

Esther is taken to the king in the tenth month, in the seventh year of the king's reign. The number ten suggests "having to do with kingdom": The Ten Commandments are the laws of the Kingdom, the tithe (one-tenth) is the gift of the Kingdom. Seven speaks of that which is appropriate, perfect, complete: the seven days of creation, the seven sons of Jesse, the seven words from the cross, the seven churches, seven seals and seven trumpets in Revelation. It was not Esther's seventh year, but the *king's* seventh year. The time was right according to the will and purpose of the king.

The call to intercession presents a daunting challenge. When the call comes we may feel inadequate, unready. But this is no reason to draw back. It is in fact central to our preparation that we situate no trust in ourselves, but only in the presence, guidance and power of the Holy Spirit. This was the triumphant testimony of the apostle Paul in the face of *unanswered prayer!* Three times he pleaded with the Lord about a thorn that was given him in the flesh, that it should leave him, but it did not (see 2 Corinthians 12:7–8). Then he proclaimed,

> It is central to our preparation that we situate no trust in ourselves, but only in the presence, guidance and power of the Holy Spirit.

> I will boast all the more gladly of my weaknesses, so that the power of Christ may rest upon me. For the sake of Christ, then, I am content with weaknesses, insults, hardships, persecutions, and calamities. For when I am weak, then I am strong. (verses 9–10)

The intercessor moves into ministry despite weakness and fear because the call has come. For God the time is right; that is what counts. God's Word is more to be reckoned with than one's personal desire, disinclination or fear. "My grace is sufficient for you, for my power is made perfect in weakness" (2 Corinthians 12:9).

As the story of Esther unfolds, her call to intercede with the king becomes a matter of life and death.

> The intercessor moves into ministry despite weakness and fear because the call has come.

52

Yet even at the outset, the intercessor must deal with any spirit of reluctance or foot-dragging lest one become another Vashti. "Oh! I am not ready. I cannot come. It is not convenient."

> God's Word is more to be reckoned with than one's personal desire, disinclination or fear.

The intercessor's primary concern is to please the Lord. When that prevails, the power and blessing of heaven are released on earth.

> The king loved Esther more than all the women, and she won grace and favor in his sight more than all the virgins, so that he set the royal crown on her head and made her queen instead of Vashti. Then the king gave a great feast for all his officials and servants; it was Esther's feast. He also granted a remission of taxes to the provinces and gave gifts with royal generosity. (Esther 2:17–18)

This is beautiful. Who declares remission of taxes and distributes gifts with royal generosity? The king. And why? Because he is delighted in his bride. Speaking at a national leaders conference of the Catholic charismatic renewal in Ann Arbor, Michigan, some years ago, Jim Cavanar struck a fundamental note of New Testament thought in regard to the Church's presence in the world: "Building up the Body of Christ is itself a service to the world." When the Bride is prepared, when the Bride delights the Bridegroom, the Bridegroom releases bounty to the world.

> The intercessor's primary concern is to please the Lord. When that prevails, the power and blessing of heaven are released on earth.

> When the Church pleases God, God in His delight turns to bless the world.

The Church's first calling is to be and behave like a Bride. The greatest thing we can do for the world is please God. Esther does not storm into the corridors of the palace with shrill opinions and moral directives on the administration of the kingdom. When the Church careens through public streets expecting a din of dire pronouncements to gain hearing with the powerful, she too easily slips away from her essential calling—to draw close to the Lord, to be and behave like a Bride.

This does not mean the Church becomes inactive in the world, but it speaks trenchantly of the *spirit* in which the Church radiates a presence in the world. The spirit of the Bride must inform the presence and every work of the Church in the world. The Church blesses the world as she pleases and delights God, not as she blusters out and tries to please or remake the world. The Bride must always be, as it were, protected by and accompanied by the Bridegroom because He alone can truly bless the world. When the Church pleases God, God in His delight turns to bless the world.

Intercession Begins

> Esther had not made known her kindred or her people, as Mordecai had commanded her, for Esther obeyed Mordecai just as when she was brought up by him. (Esther 2:20)

In the typology of the story, Mordecai represents Christ as he identifies with God's people in the world, particularly in their suffering. The relationship between Esther and Mordecai depicts the intimate relationship between the intercessor and the suffering Church. A spirituality that gets ensnared by sweet feelings, losing touch with the cross, has relinquished its identity. When people exclaim superficially, "Oh, I just love to pray!" one suspects they have not entered seriously into the life of intercession. Prayer is hard work. It is a blessed work, but it is demanding and precarious because the Church on earth is a Church that must "be able to stand against the schemes of the devil" (Ephesians 6:11).

Esther remains bound in love and obedience to Mordecai. And now Mordecai brings an unexpected matter to Esther's attention. He overhears Bigthana and Teresh, two of the king's eunuchs, plotting to assassinate the king. "He told it to Queen Esther, and Esther told the king in the name of Mordecai. When the affair was investigated and found to be so, the men were both hanged on the gallows. And it was recorded in the book of the chronicles in the presence of the king" (Esther 2:22–23). Here is Esther's first task or work: Mordecai reports something to her and she presents it to the king in the name of Mordecai. It points the way to her calling as an intercessor. Intercessors pray *in the name of Jesus*. That is, representing Jesus they present petitions to God the Father.

Esther's first intercession is for the well-being of the king, not for some personal need. That will come in time, but her first intercession is for the kingdom. Jesus taught His disciples to begin their petitions, "Your kingdom come" (Luke 11:2). When this is the

> Prayer is hard work.
> It is a blessed work.

55

> Esther's first intercession is for the well-being of the king, not for some personal need. That will come in time, but her first intercession is for the kingdom.

beginning point for an intercessor, the promise follows: "All these things will be given to you as well" (Matthew 6:33, NIV). The concern of the intercessor begins, and, as we shall see, never loses sight of the well-being of the Kingdom of God. In Jesus' name, as His representative, the intercessor speaks to God concerning the well-being of the Kingdom. Esther never veers from this perspective. As the story unfolds, when her own life and the life of her people hang in the balance, her intercession remains steadfastly fixed on the welfare of the kingdom.

3

The Mystery of Evil

Chapter three introduces a startling reality into Esther's story. She is confronted with an enemy, hate-filled and powerful. It dominates her story from this point on, driving her to intercede with the king. Chapter one laid a foundation for intercession in "The Awesome Sovereignty of God." Chapter two followed with a certain natural logic, describing "The Training of an Intercessor." Now, the intercessor must come to grips with an unexpected reality that outstrips human logic and understanding—the presence and power of evil that enjoys some kind of standing with God. Not evil in the abstract, a description of something bad, but a supernatural power poised to hurt and destroy.

> Esther's enemy dominates her story from this point on, driving her to intercede with the king.

The reality of spiritual conflict moves the ministry of intercession beyond the realm of natural events; the way ahead is overshadowed by the mysterious presence of evil. The Greek word *mustérion*, translated "mystery," means a secret too profound for human ingenuity to figure out. The truth concerning it must be revealed by God. Human reason has no footing here; the intercessor must learn to rely on the revelation of God. No one can enter deeply into the life of prayer without coming to grips with the mystery of evil.

The Mysterious Relationship between God and Satan

> King Ahasuerus promoted Haman the Agagite . . . above all the officials who were with him. And all the king's servants who were at the king's gate bowed down and paid homage to Haman, for the king had so commanded concerning him. But Mordecai did not bow down or pay homage. . . . And when Haman saw that Mordecai did not bow down or pay homage to him, Haman was filled with fury. (Esther 3:1–2, 5)

In the typology of Esther's story, Haman represents the power of evil. The name Haman means "celebrated." He covets high honor. He is the sworn enemy of any who withhold their homage, who do not acknowledge the honor conferred on him by the king. Haman descends from Agag, a king of the Amalekites. Throughout Scripture, Amalekites are the foe of God's people. They opposed Israel's entrance into

Canaan, the land promised them by God. A Jewish rabbi once spoke to our congregation, telling how Jews celebrate the Feast of Purim, which has its roots in the book of Esther. "When Haman comes on stage," he said, "we hiss and boo with all our might. Haman is a stand-in for every persecutor of Jews from ancient Persia to Nazi Germany. He represents everything that is evil. He is the Satan-figure."

> The reality of spiritual conflict moves the ministry of intercession beyond the realm of natural events; the way ahead is overshadowed by the mysterious presence of evil.

Haman's role in the story of Esther is similar to the portrayal of Satan in Scripture. In the book of Job, Satan strolls confidently into the council of God along with other heavenly beings. God speaks to him respectfully, seeming to hold him in some regard (see Job 1:4–12). In the prophecy of Zechariah, Satan stands in the council of heaven, accusing Joshua the high priest before God (see Zechariah 3:1). In the New Testament, "the mystery of iniquity" is portrayed as a time when evil is at work with divine permission, though its days are numbered (2 Thessalonians 2:7, KJV). At a God-appointed hour the mystery will be "finished" (Revelation 10:7, KJV); the "accuser of our brothers" will be thrown down (Revelation 12:10). In the present time, the relationship between God and Satan is adversarial, yet not openly hostile. Satan takes being "celebrated" as his due—in the councils of heaven, and preeminently on earth. He is the enemy of God, yet God allows him a mysterious relationship that cannot be fully grasped by human reason. It baffles human understanding that Satan merits high standing with God.

> As one must depend on revelation to understand a divine mystery, one must also depend on divine guidance to respond to or deal with the mystery of evil.

It is not, however, without practical result: As one must depend on revelation to understand a divine mystery, one must also depend on divine guidance to respond to or deal with the mystery of evil while it lasts.

The intercessor does not ignore the reality of evil. "Be watchful. Your adversary the devil prowls around like a roaring lion, seeking someone to devour. Resist him, firm in your faith" (1 Peter 5:8–9). Yet the manner of resistance comes from Scripture, not from human ingenuity or understanding.

> We are not waging war according to the flesh. For the weapons of our warfare are not of the flesh but have divine power to destroy strongholds. We destroy arguments and every lofty opinion raised against the knowledge of God, and take every thought captive to obey Christ. (2 Corinthians 10:3–5)

The intercessor's chief strategy is to cultivate a relationship with the Lord: "Submit yourselves therefore to God. Resist the devil, and he will flee from you" (James 4:7). God has not yet chosen to fully reveal the mystery of iniquity. The intercessor is plunged into the midst of it, warned of its danger and power, shown how to respond to it, yet not able to fully understand the divine discretion that allows Satan his day. As the story unfolds, Esther models before us an extraordinary strategy of intercession. Step-by-careful-step she exposes the evil scheme of Haman in the presence of the king's authority and power.

The character of Haman comes quickly to light. He is given high honor by the king. To receive acclaim becomes his driving desire. Yet it becomes the poison seed of his destruction. Satan thirsts for acclaim. He desires to be worshiped. When he tempted Jesus in the wilderness east of Galilee, he began with two lesser temptations. Then, mounting his final assault, he "showed him [Jesus] all the kingdoms of the world and their glory. And he said to him, 'All these I will give you, if you will fall down and worship me'" (Matthew 4:8–9). Jesus knew this was no idle offer. The devil was bargaining with something he had a right to bargain with. Jesus called him the "ruler of this world" (John 12:31). But the temptation carried a higher price than Jesus would ever consider; Satan's craving to be worshiped was utterly unmasked. "Be gone, Satan! For it is written, 'You shall worship the Lord your God and him only shall you serve'" (Matthew 4:10).

In the typology of Esther's story, Mordecai represents the Lord Jesus, who chooses to endure suffering, even death, rather than bow down to the enemy of God and His people. It is interesting to note in passing that this is one of the subtle ways Scripture testifies to the divinity of Christ: *He receives worship.* When Thomas knelt down and said, "My Lord and my God!" (John 20:28), Jesus received his worship. When John, awed by the vision he was receiving, fell down at the foot of an angel, the angel said, "You must not do that! I am a fellow servant with you and your brothers who hold to the testimony of Jesus. Worship God" (Revelation 19:10). The angel would not receive worship. Jesus did. Satan wants to, for he knows that worship belongs uniquely to God, and he aspires to displace God.

> The intercessor, or any solitary disciple in the Body of Christ, or a fellowship of believers united in faith and life that refuses to bow to the rule and the rules Satan wants to impose on the world, incurs his wrath.

The fact that Mordecai will not bow down and pay homage to Haman unleashes Haman's fury against the Jews. The intercessor, or any solitary disciple in the Body of Christ, or a fellowship of believers united in faith and life that refuses to bow to the rule and the rules Satan wants to impose on the world, incurs his wrath. Scripture lays it down as a given: "All who desire to live a godly life in Christ Jesus will be persecuted" (2 Timothy 3:12). Persecution and opposition do not issue simply from human sources, but from "spiritual forces of evil in the heavenly places" (Ephesians 6:12). Paul called a particular persecution he had to endure a thorn in the flesh and named it "a messenger of Satan to harass me" (2 Corinthians 12:7).

Haman disdains to lay hands on Mordecai alone. He perceives that his conflict is not simply with Mordecai, but with Mordecai's people. His wrath overflows, coursing toward all the Jews in the kingdom. A single faithful disciple can send deadly tremors through the kingdom of Satan. But Satan is wily. He knows that his strife is not with brush fires of obedient disciples here and there, but with the whole people of God. Why have Jews suffered such persecution through the centuries? Persecutors have been blind to the true nature of the conflict, the fact that they were being manipulated by Satan. He is a practiced hand at stirring up hate and disdain against the apple of God's eye; he knows that a blow against God's people scores a blow against God (see Zechariah 2:8).

It must evoke sadness beyond measure, and a call for repentance, to remember that through the centuries it is we who name Jesus of Nazareth, a Jew, as Savior and Lord, who have often been the ones to denigrate Jews as enemies or undesirables. The intercessor who learns to abide in the presence of God will come to share His wondrous love for the Jews. Once I was sitting on a bench in a Los Angeles park, waiting for my son who was practicing with a youth orchestra. A woman sitting on the opposite end of the bench noticed I was reading the Bible and commented on it. I asked her what faith she was.

"Well, I am Jewish," she said.

"Then you are one of God's chosen people."

"Yes," she answered, then added with a wry smile, "and some of us wish He would pick another favorite for a while." Being God's chosen people is not fun and games. In the mid-1960s a Protestant pastor became involved in the early outbreak of the charismatic movement. It brought down considerable difficulty, persecution and upheaval on him and his congregation. A Jewish friend dropped by one day and said, "Now you know what it's like to be God's chosen one."

The early church experienced severe persecution, but in Western culture, particularly in America, open persecution of Christians and Christianity has had a long lull. Since the last quarter of the twentieth century, however, blatant disdain and persecution of Christianity has increasingly broken into the open. Early in 2007, an orthodox Jewish rabbi, Daniel Lapin, sent a chilling warning to Christians in the United States:

> During the 1930s, Winston Churchill desperately tried to persuade the English people and their government to see that Hitler meant to end their way of life. The British ignored Churchill, which gave Hitler nearly ten years to build up his military forces. It was not until Hitler actually drew blood that the British realized they had a war on their hands. It turned out to be a far longer and more destructive war than it needed to be had Churchill's early warning been heeded.
>
> Phase one of [the war I wish to describe] is a propaganda blitzkrieg that is eerily reminiscent of how effectively the Goebbels propaganda machine softened up the German people for what was to come. There is no better term than propaganda blitzkrieg to describe what has been unleashed against Christian conservatives recently.
>
> Consider the long list of anti-Christian books that have been published in recent months. Here are just a few samples of more than 30 similar titles, all from mainstream publishers:
>
> *American Fascists: The Christian Right and the War on America*
>
> *The Baptizing of America: The Religious Right's Plans for the Rest of Us*
>
> *The End of Faith: Religion, Terror, and the Future of Reason*
>
> *Piety & Politics: The Right-Wing Assault on Religious Freedom*
>
> *Atheist Universe: The Thinking Person's Answer to Christian Fundamentalism*

Thy Kingdom Come: How the Religious Right Distorts the Faith and Threatens America
Religion Gone Bad: The Hidden Dangers of the Christian Right

What is truly alarming is that there are more of these books for sale at your local large bookstore warning against the perils of fervent Christianity than those warning against the perils of fervent Islam. Does anyone seriously think America is more seriously jeopardized by Christian conservatives than by Islamic zealots? I fear that many Americans believe just that in the same way that many pre-World War II Westerners considered Churchill a bigger threat than Hitler.

If they succeed, Christianity will be driven underground, and its benign influence on the character of America will be lost. In its place we shall see a sinister secularism that menaces Bible believers of all faiths. Once the voice of the Bible has been silenced, the war on Western Civilization can begin and we shall see a long night of barbarism descend on the West.

Without a vibrant and vital Christianity, America is doomed, and without America, the West is doomed.

Which is why I, an Orthodox Jewish rabbi, devoted to Jewish survival, the Torah and Israel am so terrified of American Christianity caving in.

Many of us Jews are ready to stand with you. But you must lead. You must replace your timidity with nerve and your diffidence with daring and determination. You are under attack. Now is the time to resist it.[1]

The first response to a challenge like this must be serious intercession, intercession that reckons both with the reality of evil and with the power of God.

In the next chapter, when Mordecai tells Esther of Haman's flaming hatred of the Jews, and Esther considers Haman's high standing and power, she knows that one corridor, and only one, holds hope of deliverance: She must intercede with the king. This must become second nature, like an inbred awareness, for the intercessor: "I and my people are at risk; supernatural forces are aligned against us, bent on our destruction. God, only God, can save and deliver us." To say that intercessors must come to grips with the reality of "spiritual warfare" is not a poetic turn of phrase. It is a sober reality. Satan may use a variety of devices to get at the intercessor—to intimidate or destroy—but his principal strategy never varies: He wills to destroy God's chosen ones.

Recall again the lineage of Haman: He was a descendant of Agag. The name Agag suggests "high," "warlike," "flaming," "violent." He was that king of the Amalekites whom Saul failed to exterminate, as God had commanded him. God told Saul, "I have noted what Amalek did to Israel in opposing them on the way when they came up out of Egypt. Now go and strike Amalek and devote to destruction all that they have" (1 Samuel 15:2–3). Saul was to take no spoils from the battle, but utterly destroy the Amalekites and everything that belonged to them. After the battle, Saul spared Agag and the best of the sheep and oxen, fatted calves and lambs. It seemed a shame to waste this wealth that had fallen into his hands. Saul even offered some of the animals as a sacrifice to God (like the man who comes home from the casino and tithes his winnings to the church). But God did not honor Saul's offering. God had a singular purpose: The Amalekites were to be wiped out altogether to keep His chosen people separate and protected. Now a descendant of the king whom Saul spared rises up in Persia, his heart set to exterminate the Jews.

The Strategy of Evil

In the twelfth year of King Ahasuerus, they cast Pur (that is, they cast lots) before Haman day after day; and they cast it month after month till the twelfth month, which is the month of Adar. Then Haman said to King Ahasuerus, "There is a certain people scattered abroad and dispersed among the peoples in all the provinces of your kingdom. Their laws are different from those of every other people, and they do not keep the king's laws, so that it is not to the king's profit to tolerate them. If it please the king, let it be decreed that they be destroyed, and I will pay 10,000 talents of silver into the hands of those who have charge of the king's business, that they may put it into the king's treasuries." So the king took his signet ring from his hand and gave it to Haman the Agagite, the son of Hammedatha, the enemy of the Jews. And the king said to Haman, "The money is given to you, the people also, to do with them as it seems good to you." (Esther 3:7–11)

In Scripture, the number twelve suggests government and order. Esther went through twelve months of preparation before her audience with the king. Now Haman mounts his evil counterpart: They cast Pur before him. Pur would disclose a propitious time to strike the people of Mordecai. The twelfth month was chosen. Occult and worldly authorities parade counterfeits for virtually everything related to life

> Some mistakenly think that anything "spiritual" must be good and wonderful. They do not realize that in the spiritual realm you encounter two realities: the dark and the light.

in the Spirit. Scripture promises the gift of prophecy; the occult hawks tea leaves, palm reading, Ouija boards and casting lots. In the early Church, divine revelation stood up against a host of gnostic heresies (humanly concocted ideas or ideologies claiming to be true); present-day gnostics goose-step under the banner of the latest *ism* kindled by Satan. The strictures of political correctness ape the apostolic word, "Walk in a manner worthy of the calling to which you have been called, with all humility and gentleness, with patience, bearing with one another in love" (Ephesians 4:1–2).

Our secular age has ridiculed the devil out of existence. He is a little man who runs around in red underwear brandishing a pitchfork. You laugh at him. You do not take him seriously. Thus, when people newly respond to the Lord, and enter into life in the Spirit, some mistakenly think that anything "spiritual" must be good and wonderful. They do not realize that in the spiritual realm you encounter two realities: the dark and the light. The gospel of John portrays the coming of Jesus, and life itself, as a battle between light and darkness, good and evil.

The conspicuous climb of the occult out of the pit of obscurity reminds believers of a basic responsibility of the intercessor: *spiritual warfare.* A primary work of the intercessor is to stand strong, not simply against flesh and blood, but against the schemes of the devil (see Ephesians

6:11). As the story moves forward, Esther displays a remarkable strategy for doing battle with the power of evil pitted against her.

Haman's charge against the Jews is vague: "There is a certain people . . . Their laws are different. . . . It is not to the king's profit to tolerate them." This is a typical ploy of Satan: Stir up a gossip of vague charges, innuendo that hangs out in the shadows, playing upon our fears and prejudices.

Some years ago, without any apparent collaboration, I began to receive input about a particular man I knew, a pastor—letters, conversations, long-distance telephone calls. They raised questions about his ministry. Terrible things were going on, so I was told. I learned something about gossip: If gossip finds a welcoming place in you—if your heart willingly tolerates it, listens to morsels of detail without checking it out—it gains a foothold. The accusations continued to come, from a variety of unrelated sources. I began to have doubts about this man's ministry until finally it became so intensive that a red flag went up inside me. I began to check it out. I called back a few people who had spoken to me. I asked exactly what they had by way of fact. As I pursued the thing, it was like trying to nail a shingle on a fog bank. It kept retreating, retreating. I could not seem to arrive at anything specific. When I finally trailed it down to a core of reality, the stories seemed to be based on the testimony of two people who wandered into a prayer meeting, whose names no one could remember. This is a typical tactic of Satan, seeking to undermine the work of God by innuendo and vague generalities.

The Strategy of the Intercessor

> An edict, according to all that Haman commanded, was writ-
> ten to the king's satraps and to the governors over all the prov-
> inces and to the officials of all the peoples, to every province
> in its own script and every people in its own language. It was
> written in the name of King Ahasuerus and sealed with the
> king's signet ring ... with instruction to destroy, to kill, and to
> annihilate all Jews, young and old, women and children, in one
> day, the thirteenth day of the twelfth month. (Esther 3:12–13)

A time element is written into the royal decree. It cannot
be executed until the thirteenth day of the twelfth month.
When God allows evil to test His people, He often stipulates
a time frame. It allows time for intercession. This is part of the
mystery of evil. God allows evil to have its day against us, but
He appoints the day. He proscribes limits. When Peter said he
would never deny Christ, Jesus responded, "Satan demanded
to have [all of] you, that he might sift [all of] you like wheat,
but I have prayed for you [Peter] that your faith may not fail.
And when you have turned again, strengthen your brothers"
(Luke 22:31–32). Satan demanded the right to sift the disciples,
to try their faith. God allowed it. But He circumscribed it.
He appointed the time, and through Jesus' intercession Peter
could ultimately overcome it, and then turn to strengthen the
other disciples. This is God's ultimate purpose when He allows
a time of testing. He wills us to triumph over evil.

> The couriers went out hurriedly by order of the king, and
> the decree was issued in Susa the citadel. And the king and
> Haman sat down to drink, but the city of Susa was thrown
> into confusion. (Esther 3:15)

The king and Haman sit down to a friendly mealtime. The mystery of evil attains its apex. Satan is under God's authority, he opposes the people and the work of God, yet God allows him a certain standing and privilege. God appears to be virtually the dupe of Satan, and it is the job of the intercessor to bring this to light. People who enter the life of prayer, and do not appreciate the mystery of evil, can easily go off on a tangent in trying to mount battle against the evil. An intercessor does not swagger into spiritual warfare mouthing brash rebukes against Satan, but trusts in what the Lord will do. When the archangel Michael contended with Satan for the body of Moses, he did not presume to bring a slandering accusation against him. He said, "The Lord rebuke you" (Jude 9). The Lord would take care of it. It does not mean that we fail to recognize or resist Satan, but we pursue a unique strategy. We do not indulge in fleshly invective against Satan, come against him with a stream of rude speech for which Scripture gives no warrant. The intercessor follows a different strategy. In the next two chapters, watch how Esther moves with great care and determination to draw close to the king. She does not attempt to deal with Haman directly, but implores the king to do so. The last clause in the chapter portrays the puzzlement of anyone who has wrestled with the mystery of evil. The city of Susa was bewildered, thrown into confusion at this order of the king, and the authority granted to Haman (see Esther 3:15). The mystery of evil . . .

> We do not indulge in fleshly invective against Satan, come against him with a stream of rude speech for which Scripture gives no warrant. The intercessor follows a different strategy.

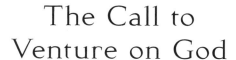

4

The Call to Venture on God

God's People in Distress

This chapter concludes Esther's preparation and thrusts upon her a call to intercede with the king at the risk of her life.

When Mordecai learned all that had been done, Mordecai tore his clothes and put on sackcloth and ashes, and went out into the midst of the city, and he cried out with a loud and bitter cry. He went up to the entrance of the king's gate, for no one was allowed to enter the king's gate clothed in sackcloth. And in every province, wherever the king's command and his decree reached, there was great mourning

among the Jews, with fasting and weeping and lamenting.
(Esther 4:1–3)

Mordecai weeps and wails with his people who have come into extreme distress. He stands outside the gate, cut off from the king. In the typology of the story, Mordecai represents Christ as he identifies with the plight of his people—suffering, forsaken, abandoned. This is what it feels like when the enemy presses his attack. "My God, my God, why have you forsaken me?" (Matthew 27:46). Jesus' cry from the cross was a cry of distress, but note that it was not a cry of despair or unbelief, for the Scripture He spoke from the cross goes on to say, "In you our fathers trusted; they trusted, and you delivered them" (Psalm 22:4).

The intercessor draws on the knowledge that Christ identifies with His suffering Church. When Jesus was on earth, He "offered up prayers and supplications, with loud cries and tears, to him who was able to save him from death" (Hebrews 5:7). He continues to live on earth in His Body, the Church, sharing the suffering of His people. In time of distress, His words spell comfort and encouragement; He shares our distress: "And behold, I am with you always" (Matthew 28:20). His people lay claim to the promise imbedded in His cry from the cross, "My God, my God, why have you forsaken me? . . . Kingship belongs to the LORD, and he rules over the nations. . . . Before him shall bow all who go down to the dust, even the one who could not keep himself alive. . . . They shall come and proclaim his righteousness to a people yet unborn" (Psalm 22:1, 28–31). The ministry of intercession pursues the mercy of the Lord in the face of distress, yet also lifts its eyes to a wider

horizon than the present peril. Scripture encourages believers to look "to
Jesus, the founder and perfecter of our
faith, who for the joy that was set before him endured the cross, despising
the shame, and is seated at the right
hand of the throne of God" (Hebrews
12:2). Faith looks beyond present suffering to victory deeply rooted in the
purposes of God.

> The ministry of intercession pursues the mercy of the Lord in the face of distress, yet also lifts its eyes to a wider horizon than the present peril.

Mordecai calls for Esther to intercede. Nothing other and
nothing less will avail.

> When Esther's young women and her eunuchs came and
> told her, the queen was deeply distressed. She sent garments
> to clothe Mordecai, so that he might take off his sackcloth,
> but he would not accept them. (Esther 4:4)

Mordecai would not accept a response that fell short of
dealing with the real issue. Setting aside his sackcloth would
not cancel the decree Haman had sent out. When people
come into great distress, or oppressive attack, well-meaning
friends sometimes offer counsel or slogans to turn aside from
the problem and proceed on with a stiff upper lip. The Spirit
may on occasion use such a ploy, but as an interim strategy,
not as an avenue of escape from costly intercession.

When my brother's jet was shot down in the Korean War,
he was seen outside his downed aircraft, but then all trace of
him was lost. Our mother found a world of difference in the
visits of many friends and acquaintances. Those who tried to
set aside the anguish of not knowing her son's fate, or simply

mouthed platitudes, helped but little; they meant well but approached the situation at a superficial level. Those who sat with her and waited on the presence of the Lord helped her attain a place of comfort beyond human reach.

When Jesus "began to show his disciples that he must go to Jerusalem and suffer many things from the elders and chief priests and scribes, and be killed . . . Peter took him aside and began to rebuke him, saying, 'Far be it from you, Lord! This shall never happen to you'" (Matthew 16:21–22). Peter certainly meant well, but what did Jesus say in response? "Get behind me, Satan!" (Matthew 16:23). When calamity befalls God's people, intercessors cannot be content with superficial solutions. The ministry of intercession must be attentive not only to human distress but also to the reality of spiritual powers at work behind the scenes. Intercessors cannot set distressing reality lightly aside, thinking thereby to be done with it. Trained in the ways of God, they are called to do battle against the powers of hell.

In East Germany, before the wall went down, the church lived under duress. Pastors and their families came in for discrimination; their children were shunted aside when they sought entrance to trade schools or universities. The temptation was strong to flee to the West where the children could get a good education. The church wisely saw that fleeing to the West was not the solution. The word quietly went out, "He who leaves his church leaves his ministry." A pastor fleeing from the East would not be received into the ministerium of the West. It was a hard place to serve, but that can be our calling when the Church is thrust into battle against spiritual hosts of wickedness in high places. My wife and I were privileged to travel in East Germany and share fellowship with some of those living under persecution. We saw a level of spirituality and dedication to the Lord different than anything we had seen in the West. Some people living on meager salaries gave up to 60 percent of their income to the church because they saw it as a bulwark of God under assault from the enemy.

> The ministry of intercession does not rest on our experience or faith or skill in prayer. It rests entirely upon the call of God.

The call to intercede may stretch our faith to the breaking point. We cower before the challenge of "taking on" something that seems utterly beyond us, but precisely therein lies the problem: Unconsciously we frame the question, "Can *I* withstand? Am *I* up to it?" The ministry of intercession does not rest on our experience or faith or skill in prayer. It rests entirely upon the call of God. The question needs to be reframed, "Is God calling me to intercede?"

Mordecai sent Esther a copy of the decree issued in Susa for the destruction of the Jews and commanded her to go to the king and plead with him on behalf of her people. Esther sent word to Mordecai, "All the king's servants know if any man or woman goes to the king without being called, there is but one law—to be put to death, except the one to whom the king holds out the golden scepter so that he may live." Mordecai sent word, "Do not think that in the king's palace you will escape. If you keep silent at this time, relief and deliverance will rise for the Jews from another place, but you and your

"Who knows whether you have not come to the kingdom for such a time as this?"

father's house will perish. *And who knows whether you have not come to the kingdom for such a time as this?"* (see Esther 4:5–14, emphasis mine)

Mordecai commands Esther to intercede with the king, to plead with him on behalf of her people. Esther shrinks from the thought, uncertain whether the king will receive her. If the king would summon her, she would go in an instant. But to blunder into his presence uninvited? Natural desire prefers what is certain. The ways of faith are strange to us, and frightening. "Oh! If God would only give dramatic evidence that He wanted to receive and answer my prayer . . . if He would dispatch an angelic messenger with a clear word . . . or speak in an audible voice, commanding me to pray for a miracle." God's ways are different from our ways. He leads us along ways of faith that are often subtle and indirect. The cry of fellow believers in need may be His way of issuing a divine summons, calling us to venture on God, to step into His presence and present the need to Him, even at the risk of being turned down.

The intercessor whose prayer is turned back goes through a death. Still vivid in my memory is my first hospital visit as a young pastor. During my final year of seminary, I had become acquainted with the revival of the Church's ministry of healing in the Anglican communion that dates back to the 1930s. I took it seriously. I believed it. Yet, as I went into that hospital room, I was beyond nervous; I was scared. Two interns were standing in a corner of the room. I could imagine the expressions that would cloud their faces when they saw me go over to the bed, lay hands on the sick person and pray for the Lord to heal her. I steeled myself to do it, but I could feel the eyes of those interns burning holes of scientific disdain in my back. What if nothing happened? I would be another kooky Christian, a lamebrain preacher. It would be death because God would seem to have turned me down.

It would be easy to charge such an experience off to immaturity, but that addresses only part of the problem. Agnes Sanford, a great student and practitioner of prayer, wrote, "If you turned on an electric light and it failed to shine, you would not say, 'There is no electricity!' You would say, 'There is something wrong with the lamp.' Prayers are supposed to be answered. If they are not, find out why."[1] Too easily we lower our expectations in the reality and power of the intercession to which God has called us. Too readily we shrink from risking the death of unanswered prayer, and thus hinder what He wants to accomplish through our intercession.

Yet, a kind of paradox may come into play here: Intercession includes times of disappointment. God sometimes answers our petitions differently, even oppositely, from what we hope or expect. What we lament as unanswered prayer may be an answer indeed, but outside the realm of our experience or understanding. We once prayed for six-year-old Julie, lying in a hospital bed, dying of leukemia. The congregation held a prayer vigil for her. Many people persevered in prayer, day and night. Julie's favorite TV character visited her and prayed for her. Several times she rallied, once so markedly that the doctors talked about when she might go home.

> What we lament as unanswered prayer may be an answer indeed, but outside the realm of our experience or understanding.

Then she died. There was sorrow, and disappointment also. We had not merely "hoped" Julie would be healed; we had prayed in expectant faith. Yet, alongside the sorrow and disappointment, we experienced the Lord's comfort, and the clear sense, "Your prayers have not been in vain. God's plan is greater."

The ultimate risk for the intercessor is God's response. The world, including erudite theologians, may pooh-pooh the intercessor who beseeches God to intervene miraculously in a desperate situation. Such opinions can be intimidating. But the fear of the committed intercessor goes deeper. It swirls around the thought, *What if God does not receive me? What if nothing happens?* How many prayers for healing have gone unspoken because people were afraid nothing would happen? The temptation comes to back down, to shrink from trusting in God. But Mordecai says, "Who knows whether you have not come to the kingdom for such a time as this?" Maybe you are not a famous healing evangelist, or someone with great experience in prayer, but you are here and God calls you.

Walking down a hospital corridor to visit and pray with a sick person, I have sometimes said to God, "Lord, it would be nice if You had someone here who was powerful in prayer, but You are stuck with me. I'm the only one around right now. This person in our fellowship needs Your help. You'll have to make do with me." When I think further on it, I realize that those more experienced in prayer than I, walking down this corridor, could pray the same prayer. The ministry of intercession is rooted not in our strength, but in the singular hope that God in His mercy will receive us.

The meekness that hopes only in God's mercy can be paradoxically wedded to bold audacity in prayer. The intercessor comes into God's presence in utter humility, yet with a boldness willing to risk death. When Martin Luther saw his friend Philip Melanchthon lingering away, next to death, he said, "I backed God into the corner. I reminded Him of all His promises concerning prayer and I told Him, 'I can't continue to believe in You unless You heal my friend Philip, because I need him.'" He remained in prayer until the conviction awakened in his heart that God was going to heal. He turned and said, "Philip, be of good cheer. The Lord kills and the Lord makes alive. You shall not die but you shall live." Melanchthon was healed.

Such boldness in prayer is a world apart from mere human assertiveness nurtured on an idea or principle of "boldness." It is given by the Holy Spirit when it is appropriate. A woman in our fellowship was afflicted with migraine headaches that persisted over many months. We prayed for her, but with no apparent effect. One afternoon I called on her and found her bounding around her house in great joy. "The headaches are gone," she exclaimed. "I woke up from a nap yesterday afternoon and felt a migraine coming on. Then suddenly the words welled up within me, 'This has got to stop!'" She was never again bothered with a migraine.

> The ministry of intercession is rooted not in our strength, but in the singular hope that God in His mercy will receive us.

> The way into God's presence is always through the low gate of trusting in His mercy.

Mordecai commanded Esther to intercede with the king knowing that she would risk death in so doing. Her only hope was that the king, in mercy, would hold out the golden scepter and receive her. In a profound sense the soul that ventures into the presence of God risks death; "The soul who sins shall die" (Ezekiel 18:4). The call to intercede always comes to rest on the hope of God's mercy. We always approach God under the blood of Christ. How easy it is to fall back under the mentality of law and think, *Well, now, I had a good day yesterday. I didn't bark at my wife. I didn't swear at anybody in traffic. I was tractable the entire day at the office, yes, and under the provocation of Miss Fudget's predictable call-in-sick routine. I went through my full curriculum of prayers. All in all, it was a good day. I can come into God's presence on a good footing today.* Oops! Back under the law; coming into God's presence on the basis of what I have done or have to offer. It is never so, good day or bad day. The way into God's presence is always through the low gate of trusting in His mercy.

"If I Perish, I Perish"

> Then Esther told them to reply to Mordecai, "Go, gather all the Jews to be found in Susa, and hold a fast on my behalf, and do not eat or drink for three days, night or day. I and my young women will also fast as you do. Then I will go to the king, though it is against the law, and if I perish, I perish." (Esther 4:15–16)

This is the breathless mood of intercession. "If He does not receive my petition, I will die. I will be shown up foolish, a fraud. Yet go I will. I will venture on God. And if I perish, I perish."

> I do not make this venture alone. Fellow believers are joined in the venture.

But I do not make this venture alone. Fellow believers are joined in the venture. "Gather all the Jews to be found in Susa, and hold a fast on my behalf. I and my young women will also fast as you do." In his book *The Ministry of Healing*, John Ellis Large wrote that, as a pastor, he constantly drew upon the pool of faith resident in the community of believers. He visited the sick as a representative of the Body of Christ, drawing upon the faith of the church.[2] The intercessor who ventures a petition before God practices a lonely calling, yet is girded by the prayers of fellow believers.

At the urging of Mordecai, Esther's story now moves into a new phase. She will venture into the presence of the king. If she is received, she will present her petition, but she will follow an astute strategy.

Part Two

THE PRACTICE
OF
INTERCESSION

5

The Strategy of Intercession

On the third day Esther put on her royal robes and stood
in the inner court of the king's palace. . . . And when the
king saw Queen Esther standing in the court, she won favor
in his sight, and he held out to Esther the golden scepter
that was in his hand. Then Esther approached and touched
the tip of the scepter. And the king said to her, "What is it,
Queen Esther? What is your request? It shall be given you,
even to the half of my kingdom." (Esther 5:1–3)

How does the intercessor present a case to God? Esther goes
in to the king on the "third day," the day of new hope, the
day of resurrection. She wears the queenly garments given

Each encounter with the king depends upon a fresh manifestation of his favor. The intercessor never comes into God's presence on the basis of what happened yesterday, but always on the basis of the grace He holds out today.

her by Hegai. In Scripture, garments often represent character, even more precisely, *change* in character. " 'The marriage of the Lamb has come, and his Bride has made herself ready; it was granted her to clothe herself with fine linen, bright and pure'—for the fine linen is the righteous deeds of the saints" (Revelation 19:7–8). The garments make us beautiful before the Lord. They tell of the changes the Holy Spirit has wrought in us. Esther's robes also reflect her standing with the king: The king has chosen her to be his queen.

In a fresh encounter with the king, Esther finds favor. She does not presume to merit his favor. Each encounter with the king depends upon a fresh manifestation of his favor. The intercessor never comes into God's presence on the basis of what happened yesterday, but always on the basis of the grace He holds out today. This is the difference between life under law and life in union with a living Person.

The king addresses her by her title, *Queen* Esther. This is important for those called to intercession. God's call to pray is universal, so also His call to the ministry of intercession; yet He is peculiarly attentive to prayers rising from positions in which He has placed us. Fathers and mothers have special hearing with God when they pray for their children. Pastors and elders have special authority to pray for the flocks under their care. *Queen* Esther. She is received by her title as well as her person. God regards the positions in which He places us.

"What is your request? It shall be given you, even to the half of my kingdom." This is a marvelous, virtually unqualified promise that a petition will be granted. God often begins by encouraging the intercessor. He knows how prone we are to fear, doubt and small-mindedness. "Whatever you ask in prayer, believe that you have received it, and it will be yours" (Mark 11:24).

The Prelude to Petition

But note Esther's strategy!

Esther said, "If it please the king, let the king and Haman come today to a feast that I have prepared for the king." Then the king said, "Bring Haman quickly, so that we may do as Esther has asked." (Esther 5:4–5)

Esther's first concern is to draw close to the king. She does not dash into the king's presence with an excess of speech, her petition spilling out. When the king lowers the golden scepter and receives her, she asks only the favor of his presence. "Let me serve you. Come and share this meal I have prepared." The ministry of intercession is not obsessed with twisting God's arm, getting Him to do what we want Him to do, wheedling, coaxing, "Please, God, please, please, please do this!" It is almost the reverse: We move into a place where God must virtually coax us to present the petition. Let us begin by spending time together. Adoration. Worship. Fellowship. Communion. A life-or-death petition weighs on Esther's mind, yet her first concern is to see to the pleasure and will of the king.

It belongs to the calling of an intercessor to bring petitions before the Lord, but the foundation on which this rests is the sovereign purpose of God.

It belongs to the calling of an intercessor to bring petitions before the Lord, but the foundation on which this rests is the sovereign purpose of God. An intercessor burdened with a petition has an inherent need to see that the petition is lined up with the purpose of God. Before presenting petitions, the intercessor looks for a time of communion, praise, adoration; a time for intimate fellowship with the Lord. This is a necessary prelude to presenting petitions. In a time of communion we learn better to know the ways of the Lord, learn to sense His mood, feel His thoughts impressed upon our minds and to dwell on the reality of His Kingdom. If we charge into His presence with a grocery list of petitions, breathless to gain His assent, the nuances of knowing His will and His ways may pass us by. The reality of spiritual warfare, with its attendant dangers, may also escape our attention.

In private prayer, the petitions of the Lord's Prayer (Matthew 6:9–13, KJV) provide a marvelous structure for extending a time of communion with God. Each petition can serve as a heading or theme for meditation. *Our Father which art in heaven.* This God so great, so far above us—think of it, He treads the Milky Way—yet so close and so related to us that we call Him *Father*, even *Abba*. Spend time to acknowledge and adore this God who is utterly beyond our understanding, yet closer than the air we breathe. *Hallowed be thy name.* His names are almost beyond number. Each name reveals some aspect of His character. We may draw close to Him by dwelling for a time upon one or more of the names given Him in Scripture. He is God the Father Almighty, the Ancient of Days, Elohim, the God and Father of our Lord Jesus Christ, the Holy One of Israel, the great I AM.

Thy kingdom come. Jesus knew well our human tendency to think first of ourselves. He taught His disciples to put Kingdom concerns first. Martin Luther put a fine touch on his explanation to this petition: "God's kingdom comes indeed of itself, without our prayer, but we pray in this petition that it may come among us." Where or how does God want His Kingdom to break into our lives today? What *Kingdom* concerns are at hand? Somewhat the same mood attaches to the next petition, *Thy will be done in earth, as it is in heaven.* The shift from "my petition" to "God's will" can help us surrender ourselves and our concerns more fully into the Father's hands, into the way He chooses to act.

Give us this day our daily bread. How often in the Psalms the refrain of God's faithfulness is repeated. Draw near to the Lord in a time of holy reminiscing! Remember His life on earth—how He fed the five thousand (see Luke 9:17), how He provided wine for the wedding celebration (see John 2:10), how He took care of His mother even as He was dying on the cross (see John 19:26–27). Recall specific times when He has taken care of your practical needs. That little word *"daily* bread"

> Before presenting petitions, the intercessor looks for a time of communion, praise, adoration; a time for intimate fellowship with the Lord. This is a necessary prelude to presenting petitions.

situates our confidence not in things or circumstances (which can change in a day!), but in Him who rules the circumstances. He knows every one of our needs even before we ask. This is a station that easily breaks into thanksgiving. Yet it also invites us to present without apology any practical need we are facing. *And forgive us our debts, as we forgive our debtors.* Jesus said, "If you do not forgive others their trespasses, neither will your Father forgive your trespasses" (Matthew 6:15). The wording of this petition could be reversed without losing its essential meaning: "In the way we forgive those who trespass against us, forgive us also our trespasses." Forgiveness is a way of life in the Kingdom.

Lead us not into temptation, but deliver us from evil. We ask God to be with us and guide us in a dangerous world. We know from Scripture that "[God] himself tempts no one" (James 1:13). Jesus contrasts such a thought with a prayer for God's fatherly protection. Then, finally, *For thine is the kingdom, and the power, and the glory, for ever. Amen.* As the prayer begins, so it ends, centered on the reality of God. To draw close to God, to dwell in the reality of His presence, this is the wellspring of intercession.

"Come, have dinner with me," Esther entreats. In the next chapter we see that the king ends up almost coaxing the petition out of Esther! When we come into such communion with God that He has to coax the petition out of us, we have entered into a most holy place. In fellowship with the Lord the answer to the petition is assured.

Esther admits the reality and presence of evil in her communion with the king. She recognizes Haman and invites him to the banquet.

> So the king and Haman came to the feast that Esther had prepared. And as they were drinking wine after the feast, the king said to Esther, "What is your wish? It shall be granted you. And what is your request? Even to the half of my kingdom, it shall be fulfilled." Then Esther answered, "My wish and my request is: If I have found favor in the sight of the king, and if it please the king to grant my wish and fulfill my request, let the king and Haman come to the feast that I will prepare for them, and tomorrow I will do as the king has said." (Esther 5:5–8)

Esther still holds off. The communion will be prolonged. The intercessor moves gracefully in the bridal relationship. For a time the menace of the enemy gives place to rapt meditation on the presence and truth and glory of the Lord. Worship takes precedence over petition.

Esther does not strive against the evil one. Her strategy is to expose him in the presence of the king so the king himself can measure what shall be done. Some sects deny the very existence of Satan or downplay the reality of evil, calling it merely "the absence of good." Intercessors are acutely aware of evil. They fully honor and accept it as part of the "mystery of God," but they do not engage evil in frontal assault. They recognize it, accept it, receive it, knowing that "on earth is not his [the devil's] equal."[1] The Lord Himself must take the measure of Satan, judge and defeat him.

> Esther does not strive against the evil one. Her strategy is to expose him in the presence of the king so the king himself can measure what shall be done.

In her seminal book on healing, *A Reporter Finds God Through Spiritual Healing*, Emily Gardiner Neal writes, "You must seek God for His own sake. We think we're striving to reach God, when in our hearts we're only seeking to realize His gifts. And this leads us to one of the great paradoxes of spiritual healing. Your willingness *not* to be healed, if only you can know God, often affords you the best assurance of healing."[2] God wants us to pray for victory over the powers of evil. Yet a first step toward that goal may involve consciously making our relationship with God more of a priority. The evil is real. It is present and threatening. Yet we "invite it to the banquet." This is at the core of Esther's strategy. She brings the king and Haman together so the king himself will deal with the evil one in his own way. The intercessor does not meet the devil alone, or head-on. As we have seen, Esther's strategy is like that of the archangel Michael. When he encountered Satan, he invoked the authority of the Lord: "The Lord rebuke you" (Jude 9).

Haman is overjoyed to be included in Esther's invitations. His star is rising! He prances away from the palace in high fettle, oblivious to the unfolding strategy of Esther's intercession. Those trained in intercession must reckon seriously with the devil and his scheming, yet not become obsessed with him, nor accord him more than his due. He prides himself on his power and security in heavenly places, but he is not all-powerful or all-knowing or everywhere present. He does not seem to recognize the bond of love and response built up by praise and adoration. His pride can blind him to the favor and access of the intercessor to whom the Lord "holds out the golden scepter." Esther's heart is stayed on one hope: that she can draw close to the king.

The Wrath of the Evil One

> Haman went out that day joyful and glad of heart. But when Haman saw Mordecai in the king's gate, that he neither rose nor trembled before him, he was filled with wrath against Mordecai. Nevertheless, Haman restrained himself and went home. . . . Then his wife Zeresh and all his friends said to him, "Let a gallows fifty cubits high be made, and in the morning tell the king to have Mordecai hanged upon it." . . . This idea pleased Haman, and he had the gallows made.
> (Esther 5:9–10, 14)

Mordecai stubbornly refuses to honor Haman. For the proud, there is always a fly in the ointment! Frustration and wrath wrap their coils around Haman. His joy shrivels into a twisted knot of hatred. Those who will not go along with Satan or pay him honor become targets of his wrath. He heaped derision on Job when God declared, "He [Job] still holds fast his integrity, although you incited me against him to destroy him without reason" (Job 2:3). You pay a price when you resist "the spirit that is now at work in the sons of disobedience" (Ephesians 2:2). Women who dress differently than the dictates of prevailing fashion may

Esther's heart is stayed on one hope: that she can draw close to the king.

Those who will not go along with Satan or pay him honor become targets of his wrath.

find ridicule and disdain cascade over them. A boy who says he will obey a curfew set by his parents may suffer the ultimate put-down in high school halls: uncool. Stand against the *Zeitgeist*, the world's accepted ways, and Satan's wrath will not be long in coming.

Haman counsels with his wife, Zeresh. The name Zeresh has something of a comical ring to it. It means "the one with disheveled hair." She may have contented herself to be somewhat unkempt—Haman's personal Phyllis Diller. In any case, together with some of his friends, she tells Haman to build a gallows and have Mordecai hanged on it. Haman thinks it a splendid suggestion. He'll do it!

6

The Overabundant Answer

Suddenly something unexpected happens. For a moment the story seems to turn aside from Esther and her relationship with the king. The king takes up a matter he had earlier neglected, all but ignoring its connection with Esther. In so doing, he unsettles Haman's scheme against the Jews.

Something from the past is called to the king's remembrance. God never forgets, yet He has so arranged the ministry of prayer that events and promises from the past shall be recited before Him. Part of the power of intercession comes as we put God in remembrance of things He needs to act upon.

That night the king could not sleep. And he gave orders to bring the book of memorable deeds, the chronicles, and they were read before the king. And it was found written how Mordecai had told about Bigthana and Teresh, two of the king's eunuchs, who guarded the threshold, and who had sought to lay hands on King Ahasuerus. (Esther 6:1–2)

The incident was briefly reported in chapter two. Mordecai discovered a plot to assassinate the king. He told Esther. Esther reported it to the king in the name of Mordecai. It was dutifully recorded in the chronicles. The king had apparently forgotten about it. God does not forget, yet intercessors are told to refresh His memory. "Review the past for me" (Isaiah 43:26, NIV). "Put me in remembrance" (Isaiah 43:26). Part of the ministry of intercession is to remind God about things He knows perfectly well.

> "What honor or distinction has been bestowed on Mordecai for this?" The king's young men who attended him said, "Nothing has been done for him." (Esther 6:3)

Esther had made her report "in the name of Mordecai." The king sets in motion a plan by which Mordecai shall receive honor. How many petitions have been presented in the name of Jesus? How many prayers for the coming and well-being of God's Kingdom have been prayed "in the name of Jesus," yet without apparent answer? Prayers in the name of Jesus are not lost. They may be received like drops of rain that fall on the mountainside, trickle into streams and finally flow into a reservoir; each drop raises the level of the reservoir imperceptibly. There comes a day appointed by God when the sluice gates open and power is unleashed. God receives the prayers of intercessors to use at a time of

His own choosing. What Esther reported in the name of Mordecai is about to be used in a most amazing way.

God's ways of answering prayer are appropriate and effective but often surprising. He responds to our petitions according to Kingdom wisdom and purpose, which may be different from, and indeed go beyond, our expectations.

> The king said, "Who is in the court?" Now Haman had just entered the outer court of the king's palace to speak to the king about having Mordecai hanged on the gallows that he had prepared for him. And the king's young men told him, "Haman is there, standing in the court." And the king said, "Let him come in." So Haman came in, and the king said to him, "What should be done to the man whom the king delights to honor?" And Haman said to himself, "Whom would the king delight to honor more than me?"
> (Esther 6:4–6)

Haman's wildest dreams seem about to come true. The king invites him to describe high honor, exactly what Haman craves for himself. The character of Haman gives critical insight into the ministry of intercession. As a type of Satan he is not only a perpetrator of evil, he is a contender for the seat of highest honor. The "schemes of the devil" (Ephesians 6:11) may be what first impels us to intercession, but the deeper issue at stake is the glory of Christ. Satan's

> God's ways of answering prayer are appropriate and effective but often surprising. He responds to our petitions according to Kingdom wisdom and purpose, which may be different from, and indeed go beyond, our expectations.

harassment of us is just one piece of his master strategy to displace Christ. Esther's continuing close relationship with Mordecai is a type of a Christ-centered ministry of intercession. We may be praying for a broken family relationship to be restored, but we need to look to the greater horizon and ask, "How does this petition advance the name and cause of Christ? How does Jesus want His life union with us to express itself? Is this the way Jesus Himself wants to react or behave in this situation?"

One morning in our family devotions, when our kids were teenagers, we read the Scripture, "A bruised reed he will not break, and a faintly burning wick he will not quench" (Isaiah 42:3). We asked the children what they thought this meant. Our son, Stephen, said, "It means He won't get the little dude." Christ's patience with the little dude may exact demanding forbearance of the intercessor! Pastor Klaus Hess, a pastor in Germany who became a trusted counselor to our congregation in California, once said, "Spiritual growth requires three things: patience, patience and patience. When God makes us wait, we must consider it *holy waiting*. God is at work."

Haman said to the king, "For the man whom the king delights to honor, let royal robes be brought, which the king has worn, and the horse that the king has ridden, and on whose head a royal crown is set. And let the robes and the horse be handed over to one of the king's most noble officials. Let them dress the man whom the king delights to honor, and let them lead him on the horse through the square of the city, proclaiming before him: 'Thus shall it be done to the man whom the king delights to honor.'" Then the king said to Haman, "Hurry; take the robes and the horse, as you have said, and do so to Mordecai the Jew, who sits at the king's gate. Leave out nothing that you have mentioned." (Esther 6:7–10)

Can you imagine Haman's horror when the king's word of favor falls not on himself but on Mordecai the Jew? What Hollywood scriptwriter would have come up with such an ironic twist in the plot? Without Esther lifting a finger, Haman suddenly stumbles. His hateful scheme is blind-sided by an abrupt determination of the king. God draws us into the drama of intercession, invites us to present our heartfelt petitions to Him. But He is also at work before ever we come, in ways and places outside our knowledge or understanding.

"Blind faith" is an easy target for the scorn of skeptics. But the intercessor's journey of faith includes avenues and places that are not charted on the map of one's own experience. Beyond the arena of our own experience, the intercessor does indeed treasure a blind faith that God is at work in ways and places and with people of His own choosing. A man watched his wife begin to drift away from him and their four-year-old daughter. She worked long overtime hours at the office but refused to talk about it. He prayed about it, but nothing seemed to change. One evening he stopped into their daughter's room at bedtime. As he was leaving he said, "Pray for Mommy." The next morning his wife came to him in tears. She admitted she had become too involved with her boss. "Last night he asked me to go to a motel with him." She shook her head and said she suddenly realized how close she had come to throwing her whole life away. "I told him,

'You've got the wrong idea' and walked out of the office. He'll probably fire me." It was the beginning of a new day in their family. Before he went to work, the husband walked down the hall to say good-bye to their daughter. Lined up on the windowsill of her room were seven dolls, each of them with their hands scotch-taped together. "My dollies prayed, too," she reported. "They prayed all night."

> So Haman took the robes and the horse, and he dressed Mordecai and led him through the square of the city, proclaiming before him, "Thus shall it be done to the man whom the king delights to honor." Then Mordecai returned to the king's gate. (Esther 6:11–12)

How interesting that Haman himself must lead the horse and shout the command that royal honor and homage be paid to Mordecai. The honor paid to Mordecai was more than Esther had hoped or prayed for. But it was always a destined part of her story. The honor of Jesus is always central in God's plan. Our intercessions may focus on limited objectives; God ties them to His unchangeable plan to exalt Christ. In the end the entire creation, even His enemies, will pay Him honor.

Beyond the arena of our own experience, the intercessor does indeed treasure a blind faith that God is at work in ways and places and with people of His own choosing.

God has highly exalted him [Jesus] and bestowed on him the name that is above every name, so that at the name of Jesus every knee should bow, in heaven and on earth and under the earth, and every tongue confess that Jesus Christ is Lord, to the glory of God the Father. (Philippians 2:9–11)

Mordecai returning to the king's gate is suggestive of Jesus' triumphal entry into Jerusalem on Palm Sunday. Afterward the crowd disbursed and things went back to normal. The opposition was still in place against

> The temptation at such a time is to fall back and say, "It is over. We have won."

Jesus. Nothing seemed to have changed. Yet God had caused a foretaste of His royal dignity to come into open display. Mordecai is honored in the city, then goes back to his place of mourning. Nothing has changed, visibly. Yet destined forces have been released.

> Haman hurried to his house, mourning and with his head covered. And Haman told his wife Zeresh and all his friends everything that had happened to him. Then his wise men and his wife Zeresh said to him, "If Mordecai, before whom you have begun to fall, is of the Jewish people, you will not overcome him but will surely fall before him." (Esther 6:12–13)

Haman reports what has happened to his wife of the disheveled hair. She offers no word of cheer. "The die is cast. You are a loser. You are going to fall before Mordecai." A word of prophecy from an unlikely source. In the course of intercession there may come an intervention of God, a token answer to prayer, even something beyond the immediate petition. Esther has only been concerned for the safety of her people. Then Mordecai, her foster father, receives honor as one next to the king. It is only a token, yet with prophetic meaning. The temptation at such a time is to fall back and say, "It is over. We have won." But we have not won. It is not over. Not yet. This is when the intercessor must press in and pray with yet more

> This is when the intercessor must press in and pray with yet more fervor.

fervor. When a token answer to prayer comes, it is like God saying, "Yes, I am here. I am with you. Continue." Some petitions fail to reach fulfillment because the intercessor slacks off too soon. Jesus came into Jerusalem on Palm Sunday; it was a prophetic fulfillment of His kingly role. Yet He did not immediately take up the scepter. Many things would pass between Palm Sunday and the open onset of His glorious reign.

In the mid-1960s, the "Jesus People" revival began among young people in California and spread briefly across the country. When this movement broke out among the youth in our congregation, we found our facilities stretched to the breaking point. Ninety children were crowded into a small parish hall every Wednesday evening, and we had to borrow facilities in the synagogue across the street to accommodate a large group of high schoolers. We talked and prayed about it for over a year. We needed to add a large wing to our educational building. We had, however, two unresolved questions: (1) *When should we begin?* A building fund drive started in the late spring would probably run on into the summer. It might be wiser to wait until the fall, when people returned from vacations. (2) *How should we do it?* The thought had come to us that maybe God wanted to do something altogether different. Instead of a normal building fund drive, maybe He wanted to "visit" people Himself, in His own way. We would simply show the kind of building we needed, and let people respond as God moved them. "We won't call you, you call us."

On a Friday morning in June, as I came into my study, I saw a brown manila envelope lying on the floor, below the mail slot. I opened it up. The first thing that caught my eye was a $1000 bill. Then another, and another—five in all. And bundles of $100 bills. I dumped the contents onto my desk and counted out $25,000. The envelope had no identification on it, only a Bible notation. (To this day we do not know where it came from.) I read the Bible passage, 2 Corinthians 6. A verse at the beginning of the chapter, and a verse at the end of the chapter, seemed to speak to the questions we had been pondering: *When should we begin?* "Behold, now is the favorable time." *How should we do it?* "God said, 'I will walk among them.'" We followed this leading. We started to build. There was no formal fund-raising, though the building would cost much more than the unexpected gift of $25,000. A woman in the congregation received the word, "Many will give a thousand dollars or more." A widow came to me and said, "We've been wondering when the building would begin, and I guess it has begun. Here is my contribution." She handed me a check for $1000. In the following months, many such gifts would come in. We continued to pray. Some months later we dedicated the building, debt free.[1]

> God may move in ways we have not anticipated, linking our petitions to His greater purpose.

> The king's eunuchs arrived and hurried to bring Haman to the feast that Esther had prepared. (Esther 6:14)

God may move in ways we have not anticipated, linking our petitions to His greater purpose. He does "answer before we ask," but it may be prophetic of what is to come, not an immediate or complete solution to the need at hand. Mordecai obtained signal honor, yet Esther's petition still hangs fire. The time has come to bring her petition before the king.

7

The Downfall
of the Evil One

The king and Haman went in to feast with Queen Esther.
And on the second day, as they were drinking wine after
the feast, the king again said to Esther, "What is your wish,
Queen Esther? It shall be granted you." (Esther 7:1–2)

The relationship between Esther and the king is orderly,
but not rigidly ordered. Ahasuerus is Esther's king, yet
also her husband. Her behavior conforms to whatever
purpose brings them together. She has learned to listen
when he speaks, to answer questions spoken and unspoken, to return the ardor of the marriage embrace, to share

> Psalms of adoration, hymns, affirmations of faith, words of comfort, prophetic utterance, conversational speech, Scripture, holy silence —all find their place in the life of prayer, encompassing the wondrous reality that the eternal God is also our Father.

comfortable silences when words were unneeded. The intercessor shares a life of communion with God both rich and diverse. Psalms of adoration, hymns, affirmations of faith, words of comfort, prophetic utterance, conversational speech, Scripture, holy silence—all find their place in the life of prayer, encompassing the wondrous reality that the eternal God is also our Father.

Communion Leads to "Kingdom Petition"

Esther knows the moment that is now upon her. The king has extended to her the golden scepter, a sign of mercy and love. He has received her according to her station, "What is your wish, Queen Esther?" This is the second day of the second feast. Esther has prolonged the time of communion. Her heart is burdened with a great petition, but first she has drawn close to the king; devotion to him and his kingdom occupy first place in her affections. This will come to clear and open speech in the scene that follows.

When the spirit of Esther imbues the ministry of intercession, communion with God will assume its place of preeminence. Words may well diminish even as power increases. Fanny Crosby expressed it simply and beautifully when she wrote the hymn "I Am Thine, O Lord":

I am Thine, O Lord, I have heard Thy voice,
And it told Thy love to me;
But I long to rise in the arms of faith,
And be closer drawn to Thee.

Consecrate me now to Thy service, Lord,
By the power of grace divine;
Let my soul look up with a steadfast hope,
And my will be lost in Thine.

O the pure delight of a single hour
That before Thy throne I spend,
When I kneel in prayer, and with Thee, my God,
I commune as friend with friend!

There are depths of love that I cannot know
Till I cross the narrow sea;
There are heights of joy that I may not reach
Till I rest in peace with Thee.

Draw me nearer, nearer blessed Lord,
To the cross where Thou hast died.
Draw me nearer, nearer, nearer blessed Lord,
To Thy precious, bleeding side.[1]

In communion with the Father we may find ourselves talking less, listening more. Bishop Joseph McKinney, a leader in the Catholic charismatic renewal, once made the point with droll humor, "I never used to listen to God during times of prayer. I did all the talking. I figured, I am the bride, He is the bridegroom." When the laughter and catcalls died down, he made his point: "When I began to listen, things happened. I saw new directions that prayer could take."

> To pray in the name of Jesus means to pray as His personal representative, to come into God's presence and present to God the things Jesus wants presented to God.

This weighs upon the intercessor as an inherent necessity when praying "in the name of Jesus." To pray in the name of Jesus means to pray as His personal representative, to come into God's presence and present to God the things Jesus wants presented to God. A salesman presents to a customer the things his company wants presented. He acts in the name of those who commissioned and sent him. How can we pray in the name of Jesus until we take time to know the things Jesus wants prayed? I once prayed for a person intensively over a period of a couple of years. Nothing much happened. One morning I suddenly stopped and asked God, "How do You want me to pray for this person?" It came to me clearly—something I had never before prayed in regard to that person, something simple. I had an inner conviction God was dealing with this prayer differently. I had stepped into the reality of praying *in the name of Jesus*.

Like Esther, we must learn the place of patience, not shortening the time of communion, adoration and listening. When the moment is ripe, let the King coax out the petition.

Then Queen Esther answered, "If I have found favor in your sight, O king, and if it please the king, let my life be granted me for my wish, and my people for my request. For we have been sold, I and my people, to be destroyed, to be killed, and to be annihilated. If we had been sold merely as slaves, men and women, I would have been silent, for our affliction is not to be compared with the loss to the king." (Esther 7:3–4)

Esther's petition concerns the welfare of the kingdom. Now it stands out that her communion with the king has not been a shoddy routine to wheedle him into granting her petition. On the contrary, the time has served to deepen her concern for the welfare of the king. When she speaks her petition she goes beyond the affliction of the Jews. Valuable people of the realm will be lost by Haman's planned destruction of the Jews. One is reminded how Moses argued with God in the wilderness of Sinai, when the people of Israel stood under a cloud of judgment:

> "Remember Abraham, Isaac, and Israel, your servants, to whom you swore by your own self, and said to them, 'I will multiply your offspring as the stars of heaven, and all this land that I have promised I will give to your offspring, and they shall inherit it forever.'" (Exodus 32:13)

The Jews are Esther's people, but they are also people of the king. They are his subjects and he is about to lose them. If they were to be sold as slaves, and the king receive some profit, Esther would have held her silence. "What is our affliction? Not worthy of mention. But the destruction that is planned will bring loss to the king." This is the powerful place Esther has attained in her communion with the king: Her petition has become a matter of the kingdom.

I once read a prayer attributed to Martin Luther. He framed his petitions from a Kingdom perspective, with words like these: "These are Your affairs. This is Your church. This is

Your kingdom that is at stake. By Your gracious invitation we have been invited to participate in the kingdom, but it is really Your issue." These are the kind of petitions God would coax out of us. "Lord, this is Your family, Your congregation, Your undertaking. This is Your child under assault. This is Your missionary who has come into harm's way." The petitions of an intercessor go beyond a recitation of one's own needs. They present God's concerns. Where the issue of salvation is at stake, the position of the intercessor is especially strong, for this touches on God's Kingdom, His family.

Now the strategy of intercession reaches its zenith. The king takes the measure of evil.

> King Ahasuerus said to Queen Esther, "Who is he, and where is he, who has dared to do this?" And Esther said, "A foe and enemy! This wicked Haman!" Then Haman was terrified before the king and the queen. And the king arose in his wrath from the wine-drinking and went into the palace garden, but Haman stayed to beg for his life from Queen Esther, for he saw that harm was determined against him by the king. (Esther 7:5–7)

In drawing near to the king, Esther has provoked a direct confrontation between the king and Haman. She exercised great care not to come against Haman trusting in her own power and authority. She drew near the king so the king would deal with Haman. We cannot wrestle against evil trusting our own wit and strength. God never intended it so. We are no equal of Satan. When we come into communion with the Lord, the authority of the Lord can take the measure of Satan. Communion with the Lord and the exercise of spiritual authority are virtually two sides of the same coin. The ministry of intercession continually calls us to "be renewed in the spirit of [our] minds" (Ephesians 4:23), to give up thinking of ourselves as solitary individuals, begin reckoning ourselves

> Communion with the Lord and the exercise of spiritual authority are virtually two sides of the same coin.

indwelt by the Holy Spirit, united with the life of the risen Lord. It is the believer in life union with Jesus Christ who can exercise authority over the power of Satan.

We are going to see, as the story further unfolds, that great authority comes into the hands of God's people, but the authority depends altogether on the authority that stands behind—that of the king. Satan has a grudging respect for spiritual authority. How often the people said of Jesus, "What is this? A new teaching with authority! He commands even the unclean spirits, and they obey him" (Mark 1:27). The spirits know the authority of Christ just as Haman knew the authority of Ahasuerus. Haman did not presume to be a match for Ahasuerus. He thought he could destroy Mordecai by scheming deceit, but he knew he was no match for the king.

The king goes out in wrath. The ministry of intercession reckons seriously with the wrath of God. Beware the temptation to substitute human sentimentality for divine determination. "Oh, let's not talk about the wrath of God. That's the God of the Old Testament. Tell me about the God of love." Right now I'm glad the king has wrath. That means he is going to deal with the presumption of evil, and deal with it decisively. It takes the wrath of God to deal with the power of evil.

Watch Haman's strategy. He saw that evil was determined against him. He begged for his life from Esther. When Satan sees you have found power with God, that secret place of intercession where God is answering your prayers, he will try to strike a deal with you. He will try to get you to water down the command of God. "We can make a deal, Queen Esther. I'll give you ten thousand talents of silver. You can have some of my best horses. I have many good things I can offer to you." This is the trap King Saul fell into in his battle with the Amalekites. Saul spared some of the spoil he had won in battle. "These are good cattle. We can make use of these. And some of the sheep also" (see 1 Samuel 15:9). But God had said, "Take no spoil. Wipe them out completely" (see verses 2–3).

In the course of our intercessions, the Holy Spirit may reveal areas of our personal life where Satan has gained a foothold. It could be anything—the kind of literature we have been reading, the kind of company we are keeping, the way we are using our time. When we recognize Satan has achieved an inroad into our life, and confess it to God, Satan will sidle up and say, "Well, now, I suppose some of those things have been a little over the top. But you don't want to go overboard, do you? Become straitlaced? You know, a legalist!" He will try to keep a hook in you. If he can make a deal, he can begin to win back territory that is about to be taken away from him.

> Beware the temptation to substitute human sentimentality for divine determination.

The king returned from the palace garden to the place where they were drinking wine, as Haman was falling

114

on the couch where Esther was. And the king said, "Will he even assault the queen in my presence, in my own house?" (Esther 7:8)

In the typology of the story, Ahasuerus represents Christ the ruling one; also Christ the Bridegroom. Esther represents the Bride, the Church. Ahasuerus's love for Esther is a *jealous* love. Throughout Scripture, God's love for His people is described as a jealous love: "I the LORD your God am a jealous God" (Exodus 20:5). The jealous love of Christ for His Church speaks of the love He awaits from the Church, but it also speaks of His singular love toward the Church. We need to guard our speech against frivolously disparaging the Church. Some people virtually measure their spirituality by the disdain and criticism they heap on the Church. Can you imagine someone blundering into this tense scene in the palace and saying to Ahasuerus, "Good to see you are settling accounts with Haman. Never could see what you saw in that man. I've known from the outset he was up to no good. I've always had your best interests at heart. Now, as to your wife, well, she has some blemishes . . ."?

Christ knows the imperfections of His Bride. He is in the process of presenting her "to himself in splendor, without spot or wrinkle or any such thing, that she might be holy and without blemish" (Ephesians 5:27). It is a process. She still has wrinkles. But she is His Bride. We need to guard against the tendency to think of the Church as simply another human organization. It may look that way to human eyes, but there is a mystery about the Church—not that the Church is mysterious or ethereal! In Scripture, the Church is a visible assembly of people, an organized body. The mystery is that the Church is the instrument through which God has chosen to work; the Bride of Christ, whom Christ loves. Ahasuerus takes great offense at Haman when he sees Haman attempting to get close to his bride.

The Flawed Strategy of the Evil One

> As the word left the mouth of the king, they covered Haman's face. Then Harbona, one of the eunuchs in attendance on the king, said, "Moreover, the gallows that Haman has prepared for Mordecai, whose word saved the king, is standing at Haman's house, fifty cubits high." And the king said, "Hang him on that." So they hanged Haman on the gallows that he had prepared for Mordecai. Then the wrath of the king abated. (Esther 7:8–10)

Harbona is "the ass driver, the baldheaded man," the country bumpkin. What irony, that he should be the one to put two and two together and intrude it into the king's remembrance! "Haman has built a gallows *for the very same Mordecai whose words saved the king's life.*" The gallows Haman designed to destroy Mordecai become the instrument of his own destruction. Therein lies a profound truth of prayer and of spiritual warfare. The instrument Satan designed to destroy the Son of God—the cross—became the instrument of his own defeat. Anselm, one of the medieval fathers of the Church, presented a "mousetrap theory" of Christ's atonement. When Satan saw Christ stretched out upon the cross, he thought his own moment had finally come. He could seize power. But the cross was a trap that sealed Satan's doom. It is a vivid picture; mundane, but essentially in line with Scripture:

"Having disarmed the powers and authorities, he made a public spectacle of them, triumphing over them by the cross" (Colossians 2:15, NIV). Spiritual principalities and powers have been defeated by the very instrument devised to slay the Son of God. In the ministry of intercession, the evil Satan devises against us can become the means of our deliverance. In God's mysterious providence, what the enemy raises up to destroy us may become an instrument of blessing.

Billy Bray, the nineteenth-century coal miner in Cornwall, called himself God's glad man. He was full of joy from the day of his conversion until the day of his death, shouting, "Glory! Hallelujah!" at the slightest provocation, rejoicing and praising God in public and private, building chapels around Cornwall and speaking to all who would listen about the Lord. He was once building one of his chapels. He needed money for stone and to put on the roof. He went to a wealthy man in the area reputed to be a miser and asked for a donation. After some talk, the man grudgingly drew two shillings and sixpence out of his waistcoat. Billy lectured him and preached to him, but without further result. He went away discouraged.

Then he came to St. Ives, a fishing village. The pall of poverty hung over St. Ives. There had been no good catches of fish that year. The people said, "You can't expect to get much for your chapel here, Billy. We have hardly enough to put bread on the table for our children." Humanly speaking the prospects were bleak. But Billy said, "Well, let's pray then. Let's pray for fish!" They began to pray. At midnight, under bright moonlight, they suddenly saw the harbor glistening with the backs of fish. Out went the men in their boats while the women continued to pray. The men brought in a great catch of fish. The villagers had food for their tables, and Billy went away with six pounds, fifteen shillings—more money for his chapel than he had received anywhere else. Out of debilitating poverty, God brought forth wealth.[2]

The very tool the enemy has used, hoping to oppress or deceive us, can become God's instrument of deliverance. We may experience this working through difficulties in personal relationships. Some aspect of a relationship may rub us like sandpaper. Think of a person who cannot handle having his opinion constantly challenged. He finds himself married to a strong-minded wife who has opinions of her own. If a person has not been able to come to terms with strong differences of opinion, God may well use a relationship as close as a spouse, or a good employee, to work that through until he is free to listen to the other person and say, "That is something we need to take into consideration. Let's think about that."

People sometimes misunderstand the teaching of Scripture on family life, assuming that if a wife is "submissive" to her husband, she must be inferior to him. There's nothing unsubmissive about a wife having strong opinions of her own. She ought to make her thoughts and opinions known to her husband. How else can he make wise decisions, unless he has access to the thoughts of his wife? (My wife, Nordis, would add, "And vice versa! That's what 'becoming one' is all about.") I thank God for some of the wrong decisions

> The very tool the enemy has used, hoping to oppress or deceive us, can become God's instrument of deliverance.

Nordis protected me from making by sharing her strong opinions, and some of the right decisions she pointed out! When we were first married, I tended to react to something that looked preposterous with a knee-jerk, "Impossible. We can't do that."

> Esther has now prevailed against her oppressor. But the story is not over yet.

We made a number of trips to Europe during our summer vacations because our congregation was developing important contacts with groups in Germany. Around March the "rocket" would fire off. I would be sitting down for lunch and Nordis would say, "I think we need to go to Europe this summer." "Impossible! We can't do it. We don't have time. We don't have the money." We always went. I learned, when those "rockets" went off, to shudder inwardly and say, "Let's think about that." Something wonderful happens when you step back and give the Holy Spirit a chance to speak into a situation. It is like the old axiom of "counting to ten." A person who is short-tempered is told to count to ten before he speaks so the natural reaction can step to the side and another thought gain hearing. The Spirit is often the quiet one, evoking the bridal nature. He does not usually interrupt and shout, but comes quietly alongside and presents another side of the truth.

Esther has now prevailed against her oppressor. The evil he planned against her and her people has been turned to his own destruction. But the story is not over yet.

Part Three

THE TRIUMPH
OF
INTERCESSION

8

The Righteous
Receive Authority

On that day King Ahasuerus gave to Queen Esther the house of Haman, the enemy of the Jews. And Mordecai came before the king, for Esther had told what he was to her. And the king took off his signet ring, which he had taken from Haman, and gave it to Mordecai. And Esther set Mordecai over the house of Haman. (Esther 8:1–2)

In the typology of Esther's story, "the house of Haman" is the earth on which we live. Jesus called Satan "the prince of this world" (John 12:31, NIV). But he is a usurping prince. Jesus came to take back authority over the earth. "All authority in heaven and on earth has been given to me" (Matthew 28:18).

Mordecai is set over the house of Haman. Esther enters into more than she dreamed of when she first became an intercessor. When God puts a call upon your life, He has more in mind than you realize. David du Plessis was a pastor and evangelist, little known outside the Pentecostal circles of South Africa into which he was born. One day he sensed the Lord telling him to visit offices of the World Council of Churches. He had not been raised to expect much from such a source, but he arranged a meeting with some of their officials. He shared his Pentecostal testimony with them. To his surprise, they responded warmly and set up some further meetings. It was the beginning of his worldwide ministry as "Mr. Pentecost," ambassador without portfolio to the historic churches of Protestantism and Catholicism.

I met David in 1960, about a week after I received the Holy Spirit in the sense of Acts 8:14–17. He spoke a word of wisdom that was typical of his ministry to pastors in historic denominations:

> Tell your wife and your bishop about your experience, and then be quiet for a while. Don't set your congregation on its ear and don't "run with the Pentecostals." What we have is fine for us, but it won't fly in the culture of the Lutheran church. Pray that God will show you how to introduce this truth of Scripture to your people, and then be quiet for a time. Wait for God to bring people to you who are ready to receive the Word. If your people fail to see in you the marks of love and humility, they will have every reason to doubt the authenticity of your experience.

> Intercession is necessary to carrying out the purpose and plans of God.

He prayed over me that God would open doors for me to share in Lutheran churches the truth about "receiving the Holy Spirit." In the years that followed I was able to do this in many places around the world. When David went to that first meeting with officials of the World Council of Churches, he had scant inkling that God would bring him as a fatherly presence alongside thousands of people in Protestant and Catholic churches, and that he would play a prominent role in one of the most sweeping renewal movements in the history of the Church. But it was on God's drawing board from the outset, when, as David would later write about it, "the Spirit bade me go."

> When you feel yourself drawn into intercession, reckon seriously with the fact that the Lord has discovered you and the time is right!

Intercession is necessary to carrying out the purpose and plans of God. Esther's intercession comes in the seventh year of the king's reign, signifying a perfect time, a time that has come on God's timetable. When you feel yourself drawn into intercession, reckon seriously with the fact that the Lord has discovered you and the time is right! He may begin by alerting you to something that is apparent to you, but that one thing is part of a much larger plan to exalt Jesus, to extend His lordship over the earth. *"Who knows whether you have not come to the kingdom for such a time as this?"* (Esther 4:14, emphasis mine).

Esther has presented her petition to the king, but she is not yet finished with her job of intercession.

> On what basis does the intercessor come? Ever and always on the basis of mercy.

> Esther spoke again to the king. She fell at his feet and wept and pleaded with him to avert the evil plan of Haman the Agagite and the plot that he had devised against the Jews. When the king held out the golden scepter to Esther, Esther rose and stood before the king. (Esther 8:3–5)

On what basis does the intercessor come? Ever and always on the basis of mercy. The king has received Esther graciously, has dealt with her enemy. Yet she does not presume, "Ah! He has received me. Now I can come into his presence whenever and however I please." She knows that each encounter with the king is a fresh occasion to experience his mercy and favor. The intercessor again and again and ever again approaches the Father on the basis of mercy, through the blood of Christ.

At one time we lived about two miles from the church where I was pastor. Early Sunday mornings I would walk to the church, going over the sermon text in my mind. When the text dealt with the blood of Christ, it always carried a heightened sense of reality and power. I cannot explain that logically, but the remembrance is still vivid decades later. It is a sturdy support in intercession to meditate on the blood of Christ. It prepares us to stand before God.

> Esther rose and stood before the king. And she said, "If it please the king . . . let an order be written to revoke the letters devised by Haman the Agagite, the son of Hammedatha, which he wrote to destroy the Jews who are in all the provinces of the king. . . . Then King Ahasuerus said to Queen Esther and

God's plan is bound to His unchangeable word.

to Mordecai the Jew, . . . "An edict written in the name of the king and sealed with the king's ring cannot be revoked." (Esther 8:5–8)

The law of the Medes and the Persians is typological of the law of God: It could not be revoked. The king reminds Esther of this law. A word sealed with the king's name and ring could never be changed. Even Ahasuerus could not take back the word Haman had sealed with the signet ring the king had given him. But the king is not baffled. He allows another decree to be issued and sealed with his ring, allowing "the Jews who were in every city to gather and defend their lives, to destroy, to kill, and to annihilate any armed force of any people or province that might attack them" (verse 11).

God's plan is bound to His unchangeable word. God once spoke an irrevocable word over all humanity: "The soul who sins shall die" (Ezekiel 18:4). He could not simply "take back" this word if His mercy or sympathy were touched. "Oh, I will set that aside. It is too hard." Morton Kelsey, an Episcopalian scholar who taught at Notre Dame University, once depicted, with irony, the rift between man's ways and God's way: "If I were God, I would be a lot easier on people," he said. Human sympathy readily sets aside or softens hard words, but this is not God's way. Every word He speaks is part of His eternal plan. His sentence of death upon sin will never be revoked, but it does not stand alone. Another decree has gone out, the law of sacrifice: The sentence of death can be carried out upon the head of a substitute. The death sentence decreed by God will surely be executed, either upon Jesus or upon us in the second death (see Revelation 20:15).

Intercessors Take Authority over the Power of Evil

Mordecai and Esther receive authority to deal with things Haman formerly controlled. His whole house and everything he ruled come under their authority. One of the fruits of intercession is the authority and power to deal with the power of the evil one. When David Wilkerson went to his knees and pitched the power of the cross against the power of the switchblade on the streets of New York, God gave him authority to deal decisively with drug addiction.[1] Wilkerson once talked with a group of us in Anaheim, California. He stomped into the meeting and opened with the quip, "Oh, I'm mad tonight!" He had just come from a meeting on drug addiction with a group of sociologists in San Francisco whose work had been funded by a million-dollar grant from the federal government. When he arrived at that meeting a man was reading a scholarly paper, the substance of which declared, "We have presented dope addicts with the most compelling evidence of the deleterious effects of drug addiction, but without effect. So far as we are able to determine, there is no real cure for drug addiction." Their standard: "Before you can be considered cured, you must be off drugs as long as you were on drugs." They suspended their proceedings for a time and introduced Wilkerson. "Mr. Wilkerson has been working in this area, and he will share with us his experience." Some of his converts, former dope addicts, were with him. One said, "I was seven years on the stuff, a mainliner. I've been off eight years now. Jesus changed my life." Several gave testimonies to similar effect. The chairman thanked them politely, the group went back to reading learned papers about the effects of psychiatry, social counseling and hospitalization, and intoned again, "Authoritative research indicates that there is no real cure for drug addiction." With a sad shake of his head Wilkerson said to our group, "They won't recognize our work because we don't use their methods." The former addicts had experienced authority of a different kind than appealed to the academics.

Behind Mordecai and Esther's power to execute judgment stands the full authority of the king. The church fathers spoke of "the power of the keys." Jesus said, "I will give you the keys of the kingdom of heaven, and whatever you bind on earth shall be bound in heaven, and whatever you loose on earth shall be loosed in heaven" (Matthew 16:19). God's people have authority to deal with the power of evil, but it is not lodged in a verbal formula that they use at their own discretion. We have seen the place Scripture gives to prayer "in the name of Jesus"; that also is more than a verbal formula. Tacking "in the name of Jesus" on the end of a self-chosen, self-serving prayer adds five words to the prayer, nothing more. Intercession truly prayed "in the name of Jesus" represents Jesus to the Father, He to whom "all authority in heaven and on earth has been given" (Matthew 28:18). The intercessor in life union with Jesus Christ has authority to execute judgment upon the power of evil.

The king allowed the Jews who were in every city to gather and defend their lives, to destroy, to kill, and to annihilate any armed force of any people or province that might attack them. . . . Then Mordecai went out from the presence of the king in royal

> The intercessor in life-union with Jesus Christ has authority to execute judgment upon the power of evil.

robes of blue and white, with a great golden crown and a robe of fine linen and purple, and the city of Susa shouted and rejoiced. (Esther 8:11, 15)

When Christ comes to royal power, among His people there is a swelling of faith and hope and expectation. The intercessor dwells upon Christ's victory, meditates deeply upon His exaltation to the right hand of the Father. This is the goal of intercession: to come to a place where we see the glory of Christ triumph over the power of the enemy. On a trip to England, my wife and I met Eric Hoffer, a gifted evangelist. He told us how he had prayed for his gloomy, skeptical father-in-law for more than thirty years. "A month before he died, the old buzzard finally came to faith! He was a picture of joy. He witnessed to everybody who came to visit him in the hospital. 'Why are you looking so sad?' he would say. 'I've met Jesus. I know where I'm going. What about you?'"

The Jews had light and gladness and joy and honor. And in every province and in every city, wherever the king's command and his edict reached, there was gladness and joy among the Jews, a feast and a holiday. And many from the peoples of the country declared themselves Jews, for fear of the Jews had fallen on them. (Esther 8:16–17)

> Victory in prayer is cause for celebration. But it can become a distraction. There is a greater cause for celebration: Rejoice that you have been saved by the King.

They experience great joy, even though they still have not dealt with the problem. For now they have the expectation of victory, a victory rooted in the king's decision to save their lives. When Jesus sent 72 disciples on a mission, they returned with joy. "Lord, even the demons are subject to us in your name!" Jesus rejoiced with them, but He also cautioned them, "Nevertheless, do not rejoice in this, that the spirits are subject to you, but rejoice that your names are written in heaven" (Luke 10:17, 20). Victory in prayer is cause for celebration. But it can become a distraction. There is a greater cause for celebration: Rejoice that you have been saved by the King.

9

The Rooting Out of Evil by Royal Edict

On the thirteenth day of the [twelfth month], . . . the very day when the enemies of the Jews hoped to gain the mastery over them, the reverse occurred: the Jews gained mastery over those who hated them. . . . No one could stand against them, for the fear of them had fallen on all peoples. All the officials . . . also helped the Jews. . . . For Mordecai was great in the king's house, and his fame spread throughout all the provinces. (Esther 9:1–4)

In the typology of the story, the "officials" represent the hosts of heaven that come to the aid of God's people when they receive authority to execute divine edict; by the same decree

133

the powers of darkness are thrown into confusion in fear of the authority of the Lord. In the spiritual realm, the "fear of the Lord" is no mere poetic phrase. It is a holy awe and obedience before the One seated "at his right hand in the heavenly places, far above all rule and authority and power and dominion, and above every name that is named, not only in this age but also in the one to come" (Ephesians 1:20–21). The apostle Paul depicts the authority of Christ breaking into public view at the end of the age: "At the name of Jesus every knee should bow, in heaven and on earth and under the earth, and every tongue confess that Jesus Christ is Lord, to the glory of God the Father" (Philippians 2:10–11).

Intercessors reckon realistically not only with natural events and difficulties but also with the unseen spiritual forces involved in the struggle. In the late 1950s, a small group of Christians opened a retreat center in the *Schniewindhaus* near Magdeburg, in what was then East Germany. They soon attracted people not only from their immediate area but also from neighboring East Bloc countries. The mayor of the town began to cast envious eyes on the *Schniewindhaus*. *If I can get them out of that house, I can turn it into a state-run home for the elderly. That would be a feather in my cap with the authorities!* The mayor began to circulate negative rumors about the house, hoping to generate a steamroller of negative opinion so he could confiscate the house. Stories were abroad that sick people had been prayed for at the retreats and healings had taken place. The mayor went into stores and factories collecting signatures on a petition against the house "for practicing medicine without a license." Things seemed to be going badly for the *Schniewindhaus*. Guests had to be sent home, or turned away. A small sisterhood had developed around the ministry of the house. Some of the sisters had to be sent back to their family homes. What could they do? Public demonstrations, letters to the editor, occupying the mayor's office—staple protest options in the West—were not possible in a Communist state.

Those still living in the house came together. After spending a whole night in prayer, their pastor, Bernhard Jansa, had a vision of the house surrounded by angels. He believed the vision was from the Lord, and he said to the sisters who still remained, "God will protect us." A strange series of events began to take place. A druggist in town took exception to what the mayor was doing. He sent a letter to the central committee. "This is ridiculous," he wrote. "This is a purely religious organization. Leave them alone." Some of the workers in the factories began to stiffen their backs and withdrew their names from the petitions. Before long, the mayor came to the retreat house, hat in hand, to apologize to Pastor Jansa. "I am sorry for the recent difficulty." All restrictions were lifted and the house resumed its ministry of teaching and encouragement, which continues to this day.

The ministry of intercession does not wrestle simply with problems or situations on earth, but "against the schemes of the devil" (Ephesians 6:11). The struggle between the ministry of the *Schniewindhaus* and the mayor reflected a struggle between the power of God and the power of Satan. In spiritual warfare, prayer is a decisive factor. This is not evident to common sense or reason; for reasons that outstrip human understanding, God has chosen to "run His Kingdom on prayer." War in the heavenly places is greatly affected by prayers on earth. That is why intercession can change things on earth: It deals with spiritual realities that instigate happenings on earth. Spiritual warfare effects change by engaging problems at their source.

When the Lord dispatches "hosts of heaven" to intervene in response to holy intercession, tremendous things can happen on earth. People without faith may not see this. They will not know about "a vision of the house surrounded by angels." They will simply see an unfolding of surface events. Yet it can affect their lives. The effects of intercession can spill over, bringing the blessing of God into their lives.

The ministry of intercession participates in the release of Christ's authority into concrete situations. Mordecai sat outside the gate, in sackcloth and ashes, until Esther's intercession prevailed. He was always close at hand, but he depended on Esther's intercession, not direct action. When Esther interceded, he was exalted.

> Mordecai was great in the king's house, and his fame spread throughout all the provinces, for the man Mordecai grew more and more powerful. (Esther 9:4)

Mordecai's exaltation hinged upon Esther's intercession. Intercessors not only experience the power of Christ's victory in their own lives and prayers, they also have a part in extending His victory to others through their intercession.

> God has chosen to "run His Kingdom on prayer."

We once experienced a considerable revival among the youth in our church. It centered on a program of intensive Bible study that began in the fourth grade. One of our best teachers devoted herself exclusively to intercession. She was on her knees in the prayer chapel while the classes met. A mood of joy and expectancy spread like a contagion among the teachers. "When Jean prays, things happen!"

> Intercessors not only experience the power of Christ's victory in their own lives and prayers, they also have a part in extending His victory to others through their intercession.

> The Jews struck all their enemies with the sword . . . but they laid no hand on the plunder. (Esther 9:5, 10)

The Jews, as they defended themselves, laid no hand on the plunder. This is repeated twice more in the verses that follow. The king's decree specifically allowed the Jews to plunder the goods of their enemies, yet they refrained from doing so. One is reminded again of Jesus' words when His disciples returned from a mission where they had seen God working: "Do not rejoice in this, that the spirits are subject to you, but rejoice that your names are written in heaven" (Luke 10:20). Answered prayer—healings, miracles, power over evil spirits—is sound reason for celebration, but it can be heady wine. Above all else, answered prayer reminds us that we have been redeemed by Christ, adopted into the life of the holy Trinity.

> Mordecai recorded these things and sent letters to all the Jews who were in all the provinces of King Ahasuerus, both near and far, obliging them to keep the fourteenth day of the month Adar and also the fifteenth day of the same, year by year, as the days on which the Jews got relief from their

enemies, and as the month that had been turned for them from sorrow into gladness and from mourning into a holiday.... Haman the Agagite, the son of Hammedatha, the enemy of all the Jews, had plotted against the Jews to destroy them, and had cast Pur (that is, cast lots), to crush and to destroy them.... Therefore they called these days Purim, after the term Pur. (Esther 9:20–22, 24, 26)

The ministry of intercession is not complete until we remember and recite to our children God's answers to prayer. Our second son, Glenn, was born with a defect in his lungs and lived only two months. We feared for our youngest son, Arne, when he had to be rushed to the hospital twice in his first year of life because he was unable to breathe properly. Then, when we met Oral Roberts and Oral prayed for Arne's healing, he was wonderfully healed. From time to time we recounted this event. It became a treasured memory in our family.

Many years later Arne was working for a congressman in Washington, D.C. One day Oral Roberts visited the congressman and was introduced to Arne. Arne said, "You probably wouldn't remember, but—"

"Arne Christenson—of course," Oral interrupted. "Your mother brought you to a service in Long Beach, and I prayed for you. I just got a letter from your dad last week!" (A couple of weeks earlier I had told my wife, "I think I'll write Oral Roberts, just to tell him we think of him and thank God for his ministry when we think of Arne, who is now healthy and grown up with a family of his own.")

To this day Jews celebrate the Feast of Purim, remembering their deliverance in the days of Queen Esther. They see it as a type of God's concern for His chosen people and His deliverance of them in many situations.

When the call to intercede came, Esther took her life in her hands and said, "If I perish, I perish." Her intercession won not only her own life and the life of her people, but exalted Mordecai to the right hand of the king. The glory of that event is recorded in the final chapter of Esther's story.

> When the call
> to intercede came,
> Esther took her life
> in her hands and said,
> "If I perish, I perish."

10

The Vindication and Rule of the Righteous

The full account of the high honor of Mordecai, . . . are they
not written in the Book of the Chronicles of the kings of
Media and Persia? For Mordecai the Jew was second in rank
to King Ahasuerus, and he was great among the Jews and
popular with the multitude of his brothers, for he sought
the welfare of his people and spoke peace to all his people.
(Esther 10:2–3)

This is the final result of Esther's intercession, though it came
to reality only step by step. The ultimate goal of the ministry
of intercession is the exaltation of Jesus, who shall speak
peace to the nations. You may be praying for a person who

> The ultimate goal of the ministry of intercession is the exaltation of Jesus.

has cancer. You may be praying for a family that is about to break up. You may be praying for things that are an urgent concern both to you and to God. God calls you to intercede that these very things will be touched by His transforming presence and play their part in the enthronement of Jesus.

The Mantle of Esther

The story of Esther illustrates many aspects of intercessory prayer. It is a powerful encouragement to step into the ministry of intercession as Esther did. One final observation: Esther did not trundle a random array of needs into the king's presence, things that occurred to her as she thought about her own life, or assailed her when she looked out over the city of Susa. There are times when reciting a list of needs before the Lord is altogether appropriate, but the story of Esther shows a more focused view of intercession. Esther ventured to intercede because Mordecai commanded her to bring a specific petition before the king.

The "big picture," or an immediate situation, may be

> The story of Esther . . . is a powerful encouragement to step into the ministry of intercession as Esther did.

what first arrests our attention. We see erosion in the moral life of the nation, and our own community or family is not exempt. Some teaching of Scripture confuses us or seems out of step with reality. A friend or family member is diagnosed terminally ill. A child marries an unbeliever and turns away from the faith. The question arises, "What does the Lord want me to do about this?" Sometimes it is good to step back and ask, "How should I pray about this?" This can be particularly helpful when your

> Sometimes it is good to step back and ask, "How should I pray about this?"

prayers seem to hit a stone wall. A story (probably apocryphal) is told about George Washington Carver, the great scientist at Tuskegee Institute.

He prayed, "Lord, why did You make the world?"

The Lord answered, "Little man, that is a question too big for you to understand. Ask something smaller."

He prayed again, "Lord, why did You make man?"

"Still too big."

"Lord, why did You make the peanut?"

"Just right." Carver discovered more than a hundred uses for the lowly peanut, and he transformed the agriculture of the South.

The mantle of Esther is more than a general admonition to present needs or questions before God. It is a call to bring specific petitions into His presence. George McCausland was an old Methodist circuit rider with a marvelous sense of proportion, who described himself as "74 years old in my stocking feet." When we first met him many years ago, he told us how much simpler and focused his life became when "I resigned as General Manager of the Universe, and God accepted my resignation." A generalized view of God, a view of life with man at the center and God looking on, a religion of "God helps those who help themselves" is likely to yield generalized results in prayer. The story of Esther encourages us to spacious trust in God's active and powerful governance over all things—including His desire that we bring this particular petition before Him, so much so that He would coax it out of us! Faith thrives where intercession is accompanied by a specific sense of call.

I once prayed about the troubled marriage of one of our sons. He was moving toward divorce. My wife and I spoke with him many times, urged reconciliation and continued to pray. Nothing changed. The divorce went through. One morning the thought came to me, *Don't pray about the situation. Ask how you should relate to him.* It was not an altogether comforting thought. In a telephone conversation, our son had said, "If you feel you can no longer relate closely to me, I'll understand." What would God say? I nevertheless refocused my prayers along the line of this word. For eighteen months no answer came, only the sense that God chose to remain silent. (I remember commenting to Nordis, "The silences of God are awesome.") Then came a day when He answered my prayer with three consecutive verses of Scripture: "Be kind to one another, tenderhearted, forgiving one another, as God in Christ forgave you. Therefore be imitators of God, as beloved children. And walk in love, as Christ loved us and gave himself up for us, a fragrant offering and sacrifice to God" (Ephesians 4:32–5:2). The phrase "as God in Christ forgave you" overwhelmed me. The Spirit reminded me how often and deeply I had experienced God's mercy. He did not answer all the theological questions I had thrown at Him about divorce. He did not greatly change the situation. What He coaxed out of me was a specific petition that would release the situation into His hands and conform my own attitude to a Kingdom way of life. In the months and years that followed, He confirmed this word to us in wonderful ways.

> Esther's mantle is not foundationally a description of something we "do" or "cause," but about something that *happens* when we draw close to the Lord.

The story of Esther is the record of a woman who answered a specific call to intercede. She braved the threat of going against reasoned behavior. She set her hope wholly on obtaining the favor and intervention of the king. She did not go into the king thinking, *I have entered into a knowledge of kingdom matters that I will now employ to release the king's power in favor of my petition.* Her mood was rather, *I will go in to the king, and if I perish, I perish.* When Esther's mantle settles upon a person, it is principally an encouragement to draw close to the King and there to discover His unimaginable love, favor, wisdom and power. Esther's mantle is not foundationally a description of something we "do" or "cause," but about something that *happens* when we draw close to the Lord. Esther's life, and the life of the people for whom she interceded, was transformed. The eyes of the Lord go to and fro throughout the earth today, looking for those who will intercede in particular situations that concern His Kingdom. When you draw close to Him bearing one of these petitions, prepared to present it to Him despite every uncertainty and fear, you enter into that place of quiet power where His Kingdom is being formed. That is the legacy that attaches to the mantle of Esther.

Notes

Chapter 1 The Awesome Sovereignty of God

1. *Catechism of the Catholic Church* (New York: Doubleday, 1994), Part IV, Section 1, Chapter 1, Article 3, Paragraph III, Reference #2634.
2. Henry H. Halley, *Bible Handbook* (Chicago: Henry H. Halley, 1927, 1951), 218.
3. G. Campbell Morgan, *The Analyzed Bible* (Westwood, New Jersey: Fleming H. Revell Company, 1964), 149.

Chapter 2 The Training of an Intercessor

1. Derek Prince, "The Role of Worship," *Intercessors For America Newsletter*, Vol. 34, No. 4, April 2007, 1; excerpted from *Rules of Engagement* by Derek Prince.

Chapter 3 The Mystery of Evil

1. Daniel Lapin, "A Rabbi's Warning to U.S. Christians," http://www.worldnetdaily .com/news/article.asp?ARTICLE_ID=53748 (13 January 2007).

Chapter 4 The Call to Venture on God

1. Agnes Sanford, *The Healing Light* (St. Paul, Minnesota: Macalaster Park Publishing Company, 1947), 22; and in conversation at a School of Pastoral Care, 1964.
2. John Ellis Large, *The Ministry of Healing* (New York: Morehouse-Gorham Company, 1959).

Chapter 5 The Strategy of Intercession

1. A mighty fortress is our God,
   A trusty shield and weapon;
   Our help is He in all our need,
   Our stay, whate'er doth happen;

For still our ancient foe
Doth seek to work us woe;
Strong mail of craft and power
He weareth in this hour;
On earth is not his equal.

Martin Luther, "A Mighty Fortress Is Our God," first stanza in *The Lutheran Hymnary* (Minneapolis: Augsburg Publishing House, 1935), emphasis added.

2. Emily Gardiner Neal, *A Reporter Finds God Through Spiritual Healing* (New York: Morehouse-Barlow, 1956), 118.

Chapter 6 The Overabundant Answer

1. See Larry Christenson, *A Message to the Charismatic Movement* (Minneapolis: Dimension Books, Bethany Fellowship, 1972), 24–26.

Chapter 7 The Downfall of the Evil One

1. Fanny Crosby, "I Am Thine, O Lord," *Brightest and Best* (New York: Biglow and Main, 1875).

2. F. W. Bourne, *Billy Bray, the King's Son* (London: The Epworth Press, 1937), 58–60.

Chapter 8 The Righteous Receive Authority

1. David Wilkerson, *The Cross and the Switchblade* (New York: Penguin Putnam, 1962).

Subject Index

Scripture Index

Genesis

1:27 31
49:10 36

Exodus

20:5 115
25:37 45
32:13 111

1 Samuel

15:2–3 66, 114
15:9 114

2 Samuel

5:1–3 47

2 Kings

2:23 26

Ezra

7:14 29

Esther

1:1–3 21
1:10–12 25, 27

1:12 28
1:13–15 29
2:1–4 35
2:7 38
2:9 39, 42
2:10–11 45
2:12 47
2:12–15 49
2:16 51
2:17–18 53
2:20 54
2:22–23 55
3:1–5 58
3:7–11 67
3:12–13 70
3:15 70, 71
4:1–3 74
4:4 75
4:5–14 78
4:14 125
4:15–16 82
5:1–3 87
5:4–5 89
5:5–8 93
5:9–14 95
6:1–2 98
6:3 98
6:4–10 101
6:4–6 99

6:7–10 100–101
6:11–12 102
6:12–13 103
6:14 105
7:1–2 107
7:3–4 111
7:5–7 112
7:8 115
7:8–10 116
8:1–2 123
8:3–4 126
8:5–8 127
8:11 127
8:11–15 130
8:16–17 130
9:1–4 133
9:4 136
9:5–10 137
9:20–26 138
10:1–3 141
10:2 20

Job

1:4–12 59
2:3 95
23:3–4 22
42:2 23

Psalms

22:1 74
22:4 74
22:28–31 74
95:6–7 41

Isaiah

42:3 100
43:26 98
45:1 18
59:15–16 15

Ezekiel

18:4 82, 127
22:30–31 15

Hosea

1:2–3 16

Zechariah

2:8 63
3:1 59

Matthew

2:2 37
4:8–9 61
4:10 61
6:9 41
6:15 92
6:33 56
16:19 129
16:21–23 76
19:28 47
21:22 15
22:1–9 29
25:1 17
25:14 17
25:31–32 17
27:46 74
28:18 123, 129
28:20 74

Mark

1:22 30
1:27 113
3:35 38
11:24 89

Luke

9:17 91
10:17–20 131
10:20 137
11:2 55
11:5–9 18
18:1–8 18
22:31–32 70

John

2:10 91
8:28 30
8:29 38
12:31 61, 123
15:7 15
19:26–27 91
20:29 61

Acts

8:14–17 124

Romans

6:4–11 49
8:26–27 15
8:34 14

1 Corinthians

1:25 30
10:1–4 16
15:31 48

2 Corinthians

4:11 48
4:12 48
6:1–18 105
10:3–5 60

12:7 62
12:7–8 52
12:9 52
12:9–10 52

Ephesians

1:3–14 25
1:20–21 134
2:2 95
4:1–2 68
4:17–24 40
4:23 113
4:32–5:2 144
5:25 44
5:27 39, 115
6:11 55, 68–69, 99, 135
6:12 62
6:18–19 47

Philippians

2:9–11 102
2:10 134

Colossians

1:10 38
2:15 117

2 Thessalonians

2:7 59

1 Timothy

2:1 16
2:3–4 16
2:5–8 15
3:4–5 31
3:12 31
5:22 46

2 Timothy

2:15 43
3:12 62
3:16 43

154

Larry Christenson is an ordained Lutheran pastor, popular Bible teacher, and author of books on family life and spiritual renewal.

A member of Phi Beta Kappa, Larry graduated magna cum laude from St. Olaf College in Northfield, Minnesota. He and Nordis (Evenson) were married during their senior year of college. In 1955 he enrolled at Luther Theological Seminary in St. Paul, Minnesota, graduating with honors in 1959.

Following graduation from seminary, Larry received a scholarship to study and work in the Lutheran Church in Germany. In 1960 he was called to Trinity Lutheran Church in San Pedro, California, where he served as pastor for 22 years.

The Christensons have four married children and eighteen grandchildren. When their children were small, the Christensons, together with a number of families in their congregation, were led to do a serious study of biblical teaching on family life. This caused them to question many patterns prevailing in our culture, such as permissiveness in childrearing, "democratic" family structure, competitive roles between spouses and easy divorce. They discovered that the Bible presents a pattern for family life that stresses loving care, responsible authority, obedience and lifelong commitment. The experience in the Christensons' family, and in a number of families in their congregation, was revolutionary. They have shared this understanding of family life through speaking and writing. Larry's bestselling book *The Christian Family* (Bethany House, 1970) has sold more than two million copies, with translations in more than a dozen foreign languages. David Wilkerson said, "It is the best book I have ever read on the subject." Ruth Graham called it "a superb guidebook for the Christian home."

In 1961 a spiritual renewal began in the congregation in San Pedro, as members experienced growth in prayer, faith and the manifestation of spiritual gifts. It was one of the first expressions in a Lutheran church of what came to be known as the "charismatic renewal." Larry has been an active leader in this renewal movement and has written a number of books and articles that have helped interpret the movement within the context of historic Christianity.

Larry is editor of the major work, *Welcome, Holy Spirit: A Study of Charismatic Renewal in the Church* (Augsburg, 1987). His book *The Renewed Mind* (Bethany House, 1974) also became a bestseller. His latest book, *Ride the River* (Bethany House, 2000), is a vivid presentation of trinitarian Christianity.

From 1983 to 1995 Larry served as director of the International Lutheran Renewal Center in St. Paul, Minnesota. In "retirement" he travels extensively in the United States and overseas, speaking at congregational missions, leadership training institutes, family life seminars and spiritual renewal conferences. For more information, contact:

Larry Christenson
888 Canon Valley Drive, #213
Northfield, MN 55057

Email: larrydq@aol.com

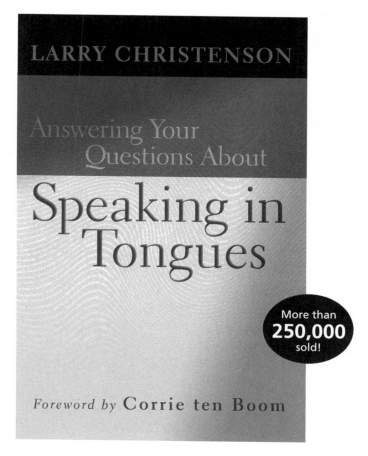